More Praise for *The Leadership Crisis and the Free Market Cure*

"Nobody better exemplifies a great leader than John Allison—a brilliantly successful businessman and intellectual activist. In this book, John shares with the world the rational principles he implemented as leader of a highly regarded major corporation and as a person living a flourishing life. Anyone interested in both succeeding in business and living a productive and prosperous life should read this book."

> —Yaron Brook, President and Executive Director, Ayn Rand Institute

"Very timely and very well written, this thoughtful book by highly successful entrepreneur and seminal thinker John Allison is a masterpiece. Our Founders would be impressed. And so would John Locke, intellectual godfather of the American Revolution."

> —Steve Forbes, Chairman and Editor-in-Chief, Forbes Media

"In his new book, *The Leadership Crisis and the Free Market Cure*, John A. Allison aptly delivers thought provoking insights by applying libertarianism to leadership. He raises fundamental questions and provides concrete advice to help business and other leaders make better decisions. This book is an exemplary successor to his *New York Times* bestseller, *The Financial Crisis and the Free Market Cure*, and is a worthwhile addition to the literature on both leadership and free enterprise."

> —Charles Iacovou, Dean, Wake Forest University School of Business

"John Allison understands business and what it takes to be successful. He also understands people and what makes them happy. He brings together this knowledge and insight to effectively argue that we should return to the principles that made America great—Life, Liberty, and the Pursuit of Happiness."

> —James M. Kilts, Partner, Centerview Capital Holdings;
> former CEO, The Gillette Company

"Weaving together personal stories and theoretical insights in his timely book *The Leadership Crisis and the Free Market Cure,* John Allison makes a compelling case for the values necessary for individuals, leaders, and societies to achieve real human happiness. These include honesty, integrity, justice, and independent thinking—all key principles for a thriving company and a humane society. It is particularly refreshing to see a businessman like Allison as comfortable discussing the Aristotelian concept of eudaimonia as he is talking about business management. However, it is even more exciting to see one of our country's leaders stand up unequivocally for the principles, freedoms, and markets that were critical to his own success and that are absolutely necessary for the future well-being of our country. This is a book that aspiring entrepreneurs, established businessmen, and even politicians will benefit from reading if they care about the pursuit of personal and societal flourishing."

> —Charles Koch, Chairman and CEO, Koch Industries, Inc.

"The best leaders inspire the people around them to reach their highest potential, and by doing so, they make the world a better place. John Allison is such a leader, and this book is an invaluable guide for all those who believe that the surest path to happiness is following your own vision."

> —John Mackey, Co-CEO, Whole Foods Market
> and coauthor of *Conscious Capitalism*

"Every serious thinker about the future of America will benefit by reading *The Leadership Crisis and the Free Market Cure*! I witnessed John Allison's philosophy at work and watched it better the lives of thousands in the BB&T organization. This is a valuable and needed work."

> —James Maynard, Chairman, Golden Corral Corporation

"Libertarianism has a reputation for being coldly rational. John Allison heats things up. *The Leadership Crisis and the Free Market Cure* approaches reason not with chilly abstraction but with 98.6 degrees of human warmth. John gives us principles of logical thinking that take emotion, psychology, and virtue into full account. And he gives us charming personal anecdotes showing how logical thinking turns us into leaders—of businesses, institutions, and, most important, our own lives. Not reading *The Leadership Crisis* would be irrational."

> —P. J. O'Rourke, author, political satirist, and correspondent
> for *The Weekly Standard* and *The Daily Beast*

"I have observed firsthand John Allison's successful application of the values and principles covered in this book in real-life business settings. What he writes isn't theoretical. He has done it with influence and impact and received much admiration and appreciation from so many. This is a substantive and stimulating read."

—Nido Qubein, President, High Point University;
Chairman, Great Harvest Bread; author; and motivational speaker

"Compelling and proven ethical leadership principles that should provide the foundation for dealing with the economic challenges of our society presented by one of the most successful business leaders of our time."

—Steve Reinemund, retired Chairman and CEO, PepsiCo

"Blending philosophy and business acumen, John Allison details how the values and principles he used to lead BB&T have wide applicability for individuals, organizations, and society."

—Douglas A. Shackelford, Dean and Meade H. Willis Distinguished
Professor of Taxation, UNC Kenan-Flagler Business School

"Have you ever wondered what abstract philosophical principles have to do with business practices and living your life day to day? Have you ever wondered what morality has to do with profit, success, and happiness? According to bestselling author John Allison, the answer is clear: *everything. The Leadership Crisis and the Free Market Cure* provides a compelling case for why success in business (and life) requires men and women to conduct their professional and private lives according to a rational moral code that will lead to increased profits, success, and personal happiness. If you want to succeed in running a Fortune 500 company, a small mom-and-pop store, or a lemonade stand, then you must read this book. It will help you to develop a code of moral leadership that is sorely lacking in American business today. Dozens of books are published every year on how to succeed in business, but this is by far the best."

—Brad Thompson, Executive Director,
Clemson Institute for the Study of Capitalism

The Leadership Crisis and the Free Market Cure

The Leadership Crisis and the Free Market Cure

Why the Future of Business Depends on the Return to Life, Liberty, and the Pursuit of Happiness

John A. Allison

New York   Chicago   San Francisco   Athens   London
Madrid   Mexico City   Milan   New Delhi
Singapore   Sydney   Toronto

1 2 3 4 5 6 7 8 9 0   DOC/DOC   1 2 0 9 8 7 6 5 4

ISBN   978-0-07-183111-6
MHID   0-07-183111-8

e-ISBN   978-0-07-183112-3
e-MHID   0-07-183112-6

Library of Congress Cataloging-in-Publication Data

Allison, John A.
  The leadership crisis and the free market cure : why the future of business depends on the return to life, liberty, and the pursuit of happiness / John A. Allison. — 1 Edition.
      pages cm
  ISBN 978-0-07-183111-6 (hardback : alk. paper) — ISBN 0-07-183111-8
  1. Leadership. I. Title.
  HD57.7.A275 2014
  658.4'092—dc23

                                                                    2014029567

McGraw-Hill Education books are available at special quantity discounts to use as premiums and sales promotions or for use in corporate training programs. To contact a representative, please visit the Contact Us pages at www.mhprofessional.com.

Contents

Introduction

THE THEME OF THIS BOOK IS THAT THERE IS A SET OF ETHICAL principles that is consistent with the laws of nature and the nature of humans that is the foundation for individual success and happiness. These same principles are applicable to organizations and to society. The principles are also consistent with America's Founding Fathers' ideals of life, liberty, and the pursuit of happiness. Many destructive outcomes occur when people rationalize actions as a member of a group—an organization or a society—that they would never justify as an individual. An important role of leaders is to live by these principles and to do all they can to influence the members of their teams or organizations to act consistently within these ethical concepts.

The basic idea is that the ultimate goal in life is to achieve happiness—happiness in the Aristotelian context of a life well-lived (*eudaimonia*). Hard work, blood, sweat, and tears happiness. This is not about having a good time on Friday night, although sometimes having a good time on Friday night is very appropriate. But happiness in the sense that when you are 80 years old you can look back and say, "Yes that was very, very hard, and I am glad I did it." Of course, you have to be alive to be happy, so there is a survival component to the pursuit of happiness.

The context that makes happiness possible will vary greatly from one individual to another and will change over one's life. However, happiness must be earned. You cannot be entitled to be happy. Happiness is achieved by setting goals and accomplishing these goals. The range of goals is almost endless: graduating from high school, graduating from college, getting married, getting a job, successfully raising children, creating a business, writing a book, and/or

1

becoming a master computer programmer, teacher, carpenter, doc-tor, truck driver, engineer, accountant, lawyer, homemaker, secretary, singer, farmer, college professor, and so on. Some people work to achieve happiness by helping others, yet this approach is still about the achievement of happiness, with just a different context. People with strong religious beliefs may strive to live a moral life based on their religion for the goal of going to heaven, but this again is in the context of pursuing happiness even though the ultimate reward may be in the next life.

In this overall context, this is a book about leadership in the pur-suit of happiness, at the individual, organizational, and societal level. The foundation for this concept is self-leadership, which is essential for organizational leadership. Most failures of leadership are fail-ures of self-leadership. And most organizational failures are caused by failed leadership. One of the factors causing the recent Great Recession and abnormally slow recovery is failed leadership in busi-ness and especially in government. Leadership matters.

There are a number of critical prerequisites for the achievement of happiness. For the vast majority of people it is almost impossible to be happy if they are hungry, cold, physically abused, afraid, and the like. This imposes a certain type of responsibility on organizational leaders. For example, other things being equal, individuals working in a healthy, growing business, family, or society are more likely to be happy than their counterparts in a failing business, family, or society, because of the sense of security that success creates. In other words, running the organization effectively is foundational to the possibility of individuals in the organization achieving happiness.

Before going deeper into the subject, it is important to under-stand what happiness is. Happiness is different than being "numbed out." Many welfare recipients seem to like (or are addicted to) being welfare recipients. However, the extremely high rate of drug abuse, alcohol abuse, and violence among this group suggests that they are not very happy.

Monks may be at peace and may have a window into another dimension. However, they are not happy in the Aristotelian sense. To be happy, you have to be in the game and playing hard. You cannot be happy living in a cave. You may be at peace living in a cave, but human beings are capable of a higher level of empowering emotions and meaning even though working toward this deeper satisfaction often entails trade-offs and painful periods.

There are fundamental principles that are the foundation for individual success and happiness. These principles are equally applicable to all organizations and to society as a whole. Having the right set of principles does not guarantee success or happiness, because Mother Nature is ultimately in control. But understanding and living these principles improves the probability of individuals being happy and organizations being successful. The foundational concept is a clearly defined and empowering sense of purpose, which will be discussed in detail.

Individuals are more likely to be happy if they are good at what they are doing. Leaders, therefore, have a responsibility to help the members of the team become masters of their field of endeavor. This requires education, feedback, and the creation of processes that support beliefs and behaviors that produce excellent results. Ironically, many individuals are greatly resistant to learning the skills that will allow them to become masters of their job responsibilities and thereby improve the probability of their achieving personal happiness. Leaders must create the processes that incentivize superior performance. People cannot be forced to perform, but they can be coached and rewarded. There is a nuts-and-bolts aspect to the achievement of happiness that many individuals and "gurus" want to wish away. Mastery of even relatively simple tasks often takes hard work and focus, which is typically not enjoyable in the short term. Achieving mastery at anything worth doing, even if it is not the most intellectually challenging activity, raises your self-confidence and your self-esteem, which is necessary for achieving happiness.

It should not be surprising that the same set of principles that are the foundation for personal happiness and organizational success are applicable to society as a whole. The Founding Fathers grasped this concept and expressed it profoundly: "Life, Liberty, and the Pursuit of Happiness." Each individual's unequivocal moral right to his own life. Each individual's moral right to the pursuit of her own personal happiness based on her beliefs and values as a free and independent person. In this book, we will discuss the implications of these concepts, why these ideas made America great, and where we have lost sight of these fundamental principles.

What do leaders do in the context of the ideas just outlined? What do you need to do to pursue your personal happiness?

1. They create and/or communicate a vision of what the organization can be (who you can be).
2. They develop and/or communicate a purpose for the organization (a personal mission).
3. They grasp the fundamental values that are necessary for humans flourishing while living and communicating these values.
4. They develop a strategy to turn the vision and purpose into reality, consistent with the values.
5. They develop processes and feedback/coaching mechanisms that reinforce the behaviors and beliefs that lead to individual mastery of their field of endeavor and organizational success. In this context, they hold individuals (themselves) responsible and objectively reward performance.

In this book we will discuss each of these aspects of organizational and self-leadership, with a special focus being on purpose, values, strategy, and process. We will then connect these principles to society as a whole, because the same fundamental concepts that are appropriate for individual behavior are also appropriate for organizations and for society. In fact "society" is an abstraction. Society does not exist in reality. In reality, there are only individuals. To take this one step further, in reality, organizations and societies do not have values. Individuals in an organization/society have values, and those values can be shared. Leaders often significantly impact the values of other individuals in an organization or society/culture. If all individuals act properly, including in relation to others, the outcome will be favorable. If individuals act improperly, the outcome will be negative. Teaching individuals (and yourself) to act properly is the source of organizational and societal success, human flourishing, and your personal happiness.

In writing this book, I have drawn heavily on my experience as chairman and CEO of BB&T, my three years teaching at the Wake Forest School of Business, and my current tenure as president and CEO of the Cato Institute. During my almost 20-year tenure as CEO from 1989 to 2008, BB&T grew from $4.5 billion to

$152 billion in assets, a compound annual growth rate of approximately 20 percent. Even with this rapid growth, we were a top-quartile performer in shareholder returns and did not experience a single quarterly loss during the financial crisis. Our client satisfaction was the highest of any large financial institute in the United States, and our employee turnover the lowest.

The concepts that we will discuss are the root cause of this outstanding performance. I do not claim that there aren't other methods to achieve outstanding results, but I do claim the concepts we will discuss will unquestionably work if executed with focus and commitment. My technique in this book will be to discuss broad concepts and then to concretize with actual examples.

Individual, organizational, and societal success are all based on the same principles that are derived from the laws of nature and human beings' fundamental nature. This book will demonstrate that purposeful, ethical individuals are the foundation for human flourishing. "Life, Liberty, and the Pursuit of Happiness" is one of the most profound insights in human history.

1

Vision

Vision is a conceptualization of what it would be like when the organization achieves its purpose or, at the individual level, what you look like when you achieve your purpose. When the organization becomes what it would like to be, it will have these attributes. In this context a vision is similar to a picture or sculpture. The Statue of Liberty is part of the American vision, representing a strong, free, open society with liberty for all. Impactful visions create emotional responses in the members of the organization and can communicate more powerfully than complex arguments.

The Merrill Lynch bull is a symbol of a strong free-market financial system in which Merrill plays an important role supporting markets. (Unfortunately, the bull was sullied in the recent financial crisis by poor leadership at the top of Merrill.) The Google symbol visualizes a free, open, and transparent exchange of information across all types of borders. In a way, it is a symbol of individual liberty. Governments with repressive tendencies, China for example, often act to stop the flow of information on Google because the truth threatens the false story they want their population to believe. Advertising often tries to create a vision in the minds of the organization's customers: Fly the Friendly Skies (United Airlines), Think (IBM), Hope and Change (Obama campaign). It is a significant error for a leader to promote a vision and not deliver. This is a fundamental breach of trust with the organization's constituents.

Do you have a self-vision? What does that look like? Perhaps it might be: "In 10 years I will be a successful [business leader, lawyer, homemaker, artist, statistician, etc.] who consistently acts on principle in my work and has healthy relationships with family and/or friends who share my values." Or it could be any of multiple other combinations. Is your vision achievable in reality? If not, you will be depressed because you are failing to accomplish the impossible. On the other hand, if your self-vision is achievable but you have not achieved it yet, what is your plan for action? How can you correct the weaknesses? Is it worth the effort? If not, quit beating yourself up and modify the vision. If it is worth the effort, then get on with fixing the deficiencies.

Let's concretize the concept of vision as a "picture" with some examples. Hugh McColl was the driving force in creating Bank of America, which he grew from North Carolina National Bank to NationsBank to Bank of America (BOA). He had a clear vision, which was to create the largest bank in the United States. He achieved this goal. When you visited Hugh in his office, he would show you his glass hand grenade. He had been a proud U.S. Marine, but there was a deeper meaning: If you are on my side I will fight for you to the end. However, if you are my enemy, watch out, I will blow you up (symbolically, I think). Hugh was not always right, but he was always certain. His type of clarity of vision was empowering to people who shared it. I personally like Hugh because he is straightforward and transparent even when he scares you to death.

Hugh McColl's vision of creating the biggest bank in America was accompanied by a number of characteristics—powerful, strong, determined, sometimes ruthless, and focused on aggressive strategic acquisitions. In fact, much of Bank of America's growth was based on very high-risk acquisitions, including the acquisition by NationsBank of Bank of America itself (with a subsequent name change to Bank of America). The only problem with making a number of large, high-risk acquisitions is that you are betting the bank and someday the bet will go against you. This happened when Bank of America purchased Countrywide and inherited gigantic contingent liabilities.

While Hugh cared about shareholders, he was not in the business of maximizing shareholder returns. He cared about employees and customers, but in the context that being bigger was fundamentally an end in itself and trumped the other constituencies.

It is interesting to contrast Bank of America's vision with that of BB&T. The vision of BB&T is "to create the best financial institution possible." The accomplishment of this vision is judged in the context of our mission, which is about the long-term optimization of shareholder returns based on superior customer service, outstanding employees, and the creation of value in the community. While BB&T grew rapidly, growth was never an end in itself. Quality in the broadest context was the goal. BB&T made numerous acquisitions, but none of them was high risk in the Bank of America context. BB&T was not conservative in the traditional sense, but it was highly disciplined with a clear focus on making rational decisions based on the facts. The resulting attributes of BB&T were reliable, responsive, empathetic, and competent. BB&T was a well-run machine that could operate successfully at 75 mph in a 70-mph zone, but we never attempted to run at 80 or 90 mph, and if it was raining, we cut the speed to 65 mph.

Obviously, I like the BB&T vision better, because I helped create it. However, both visions have their pull and to some degree predictable consequences. Bank of America became big and powerful, but it stumbled. BB&T chugged along through the financial crisis without a single quarterly loss. If there had not been a financial crisis, Bank of America may have outperformed BB&T. Countrywide may have been a great deal. (However, are financial corrections inevitable given enough time?)

Walmart has a compelling vision: low prices and excellent variety. In my opinion, the retailer has done more to improve the quality of life for low-income people than all the government welfare programs put together. My friend, James Maynard, who founded Golden Corral, had a vision of quality family dining for a fair price. He created the largest family buffet chain in the United States and my favorite place to eat.

There is a related but different kind of vision, which I will define as strategic vision. Great fortunes can be created by strategic vision. Some strategic visions may have a "picture" aspect, but this is not necessary. John D. Rockefeller had a strategic vision of how to consolidate the oil industry in the United States; in the process he radically improved industry productivity and reduced cost. He accomplished this end and in the process significantly raised the standard of living for the United States while making the automobile industry possible. This outcome was not inevitable. Russia had more and better oil reserves, but the combination of Russian government policy and the lack of a Rockefeller thwarted that country's success.

By all accounts Rockefeller was not an inspirational leader, nor did he clearly paint a picture of what he was attempting to accomplish. However, his strategic vision was so powerful that the results were extraordinary.

Bill Gates is another extraordinary strategic visionary. He saw the role of software versus hardware and the capacity of properly designed operating systems to transform the usefulness of computers. It is sad that Gates decided to abandon his role at Microsoft to become focused on philanthropy. He had unbelievable talent in software, and there is no evidence to date that he is a better than average philanthropist. No telling what major advances have been lost to humankind because Gates decided not to use his unusual talent. If he wanted to give his money away, he could have easily found many people who are at least as good in philanthropy as he is, probably better. Very few individuals have extraordinary talents in multiple fields.

Steve Jobs had a strategic vision of user-friendly software that was mobile and comprehensive. His strategic vision also had a picture component in that it is easy to "see" an iPhone and its impact. Based on feedback from those who worked with Jobs, he could be an extremely difficult taskmaster, and yet his vision was both strategic and inspirational.

Google is both a strategic vision of easily accessible, transparent information and an inspiration at the same time. Walmart's vision is both strategic and inspirational. All these visions inspire loyalty in customers and other constituencies (and criticisms from those who cannot compete).

Our vision at the Cato Institute is to help create a free and prosperous society based on the principles of individual liberty, free markets, limited government, and peace. We are the modern-day defenders of the Founding Fathers' vision of life, liberty, and the pursuit of happiness. This is noble work.

The liberals/progressives have a vision of a collectivist/egalitarian society where we all have equal outcomes. Each of us contributes based on our ability and receives based on our needs. This is actually an old vision, which has not been successfully implemented. However, they seem to believe that it is poor execution of this concept, not the fundamental nature of humankind, that keeps this vision from being realized. We will discuss this in more detail in Chapter 22.

Having a clear vision is necessary for the achievement of personal happiness and organizational success, but it is not sufficient. Vision evolves as you grow—the organization changes and the competitive environment creates new challenges. However, it is important to always have a vision in an organizational context to ensure the organization's constituencies are aligned with the vision. Vision and purpose are integrated concepts and must be treated accordingly. A vision inconsistent with your purpose will be destructive.

A vision serves as a "beacon" to keep you and/or your organization headed in the proper direction. It may be worthwhile to clarify your personal vision and that of your organization/department/family. In 10, 15, or 20 years—what will you be doing and how will it feel to be you? In 10, 15, or 20 years—what will your organization look like, and how will it feel to work in the organization? In 10, 15, or 20 years—what will America look like? If you are unsatisfied with the picture you see, what can you do to change the outcome?

Practically everyone and every organization have a vision. It may be conscious or subconscious. However, in either case, it is a beacon and you are likely moving toward it, even if the beacon is leading you to a far less meaningful outcome than you or your organization is capable of achieving.

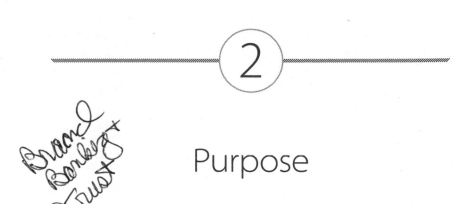

2

Purpose

THE ORGANIZING PRINCIPLE OF HUMAN ACTION IS PURPOSE. As human beings we are purpose-directed entities. In order to get there, we must know where we are going. Individuals need a sense of purpose. Organizations (businesses, churches, civic organizations, universities, and so on) are simply groups of individual human beings. For the organization to be successful, the people in the organization must vest in the purpose/mission of the organization. (I will use purpose and mission interchangeably in this discussion.)

You need a sense of purpose. I find it very discouraging how many people will describe their work as just "work." If your work is just "work," you are missing a lot of what life is about. You spend a disproportionate amount of time and energy at work. If you want to have passion and energy in your life, you need to have a sense of purpose in your work.

While the content of work varies tremendously by individual, the context is the same for practically everyone. That context has two components. Everyone reading this book wants to make the world a better place to live. In fact, I believe that practically everyone (but not everyone) wants that.

Fortunately, there are many ways to make the world a better place to live. You do not have to feed hungry children in Africa to make the world a better place to live. Businesses make the world a better place to live. In fact, one of the primary differences between the quality of life in the United States and Africa is that the United States has better businesses. Businesses provide products and services that improve the quality of life. Business is the act of production. Without production, there cannot be any consumption. Before anyone can redistribute anything, someone has to produce it. My life experience is that producing is much more difficult than giving away. Business is noble work. Those of you who are in business should never apologize for being in business. Never apologize for making a profit.

There are many other ways to make the world a better place to live. Good doctors, lawyers, homemakers, teachers, bricklayers, scholars, dancers, authors, and so on make the world a better place to live. The key is that you need to believe your work is making the world a better place to live. This does not have to be grand. You may want to open a restaurant that provides healthy food at a fair price. The magnitude of the purpose needs to be consistent with your abilities and ambitions. The key is your belief that you are making a difference.

The second component of purpose is equally important and far less discussed. To make the world a better place you need to be doing something you want to do for you. You have a fundamental right to your own life. If you were to make the world a better place but you did not enjoy doing it, you would have wasted the most precious thing you have, which is you. The odds of your making the world a better place to live doing something you do not want to do are small. So you need to make the world a better place to live doing something you want to do for you. Do not forget the "for you" aspect of your purpose.

Like individuals, organizations, which are just a group of individuals, need a sense of purpose. Let's discuss purpose/mission at the organizational level with a concrete example. BB&T is a purpose-driven business, which is expressed in our mission.

> ## BB&T MISSION
>
> To make the world a better place to live by:
> - Helping our clients achieve economic success and financial security;
> - Creating a place where our employees can learn, grow, and be fulfilled in their work;
> - Making the communities where we work better places to be and thereby:
> - Optimizing the long-term return to shareholders by providing a safe and sound investment

AT BB&T we are not confused. In a free market our primary fiduciary obligation is to our shareholders. Our shareholders provide the capital that makes our business possible. We work for our shareholders. However, this objective is an end, not a means. The next important question is how to accomplish this goal. This end is only accomplishable If we provide excellent service to our clients, because all of our revenues come from our clients.

Since ours is a people business, the only way to provide excellent service to our clients is to have outstanding employees. In order to have outstanding employees, we must create an environment where people want to work for BB&T—where they can learn, grow, and be fulfilled in their work. We do all this in the context of our communities, not from an altruistic perspective, but because if our communities do not grow and prosper, our business cannot grow and prosper.

Therefore, we operate our business in a long-term context by adding value to our clients, employees, and communities and in that context create superior rewards for shareholders.

We define *community* in a broad context. Suppliers and even regulators are part of the community. The general concept is to always try to create win-win relationships.

There are almost always trade-offs among the various constituencies of any organization, which requires judgment with a long-term perspective. For example, some clients want to pay below-market interest rates on a loan, to earn an above-market interest rate on certificates of deposit and to avoid paying any service charges even though they do not keep any deposits in the bank. The problem is that if we offered this pricing to our clients, we could not afford to pay our employees, and ultimately the bank would go out of business because the economic return to shareholders would be unacceptable. The way we balanced these constituencies was to provide a superior value proposition to our clients. Value is the relationship of quality to price. While price always matters, we focused on the quality component. Market research indicates that in the banking business clients value reliability (trustworthiness), responsiveness, empathy, and competence. We developed a systemic approach to provide this value proposition to our clients, which meant the clients who chose BB&T valued these attributes and we were able to fairly compensate employees and shareholders. One mantra I had with BB&T employees: "Never, ever sell anything to your client that you do not believe will be of value to them, even if you can make a profit in the short term, because it will come back to haunt you in the long term. Treat your clients well, and most of them will treat you well."

You will note that BB&T's mission is optimizing shareholder return, not maximizing. When free market economists and finance theorists refer to maximizing shareholders' returns, they imply a long-term context. In the real world, maximizing tends to be a short-term concept. BB&T's mission also focuses on "creating a safe and sound investment." The goal with this wording is to communicate to potential purchasers of the company's stock that we are in the game for the long term and will not take inordinate risk even if that risk could maximize short-term returns. We want to attract shareholders/investors who share our risk/return trade-offs.

Note that the BB&T mission indicates our responsibility to "help our clients achieve economic success and financial security." We should only sell products and services that help our clients be more successful. There are times when one of our competitors can provide a better product to our client. We are obligated to refer our client to that competitor.

On the other hand, the mission implies the need to be able to provide high-quality advice and to offer a broad product line. This is a wide parameter, which is analogous to being in the transportation business versus being a railroad. Some organizations define their mission so narrowly so as to miss opportunities created by changes in technology, markets, and the like. IBM made a tremendous strategic error by deciding to be in the computer hardware business and almost missing the software revolution. The company basically gave away Microsoft. On the other hand, BB&T's mission is limited to financial services where we have expertise. We do not run a railroad.

Almost all businesses have the same four constituencies: clients, employees, communities (broadly defined), and shareholders. The task is to define who the clients are and what type value (service/product) the business will provide for them. How broad and how narrow? In this regard, there is a long list of strategic questions, which will be discussed in an upcoming chapter. In a free market economy, the primary constituency is the shareholder. However, as previously indicated, when management gets confused about cause and effect, the shareholder is typically the long-term loser. Failing to focus on shareholders is a fundamental fiduciary mistake. Ironically, too much focus on shareholders (especially for the short term) at the expense of clients and employees is detrimental to shareholders. In the 1960s, the CEO of General Motors announced that the mission of GM was to "make money." Shortly thereafter GM's earnings started to decline. GM was created to make cars in a variety of price ranges and quality categories. Its real purpose is to make "good" cars, and when it does this very well, it gets to make money. At BB&T our real purpose is to help our clients be financially successful and economically secure, and when we do this well, we can make money for our shareholders.

There are a handful of specialty trading businesses that are market makers and do not have clients in the ordinary context. Some of the specialty Wall Street firms fit this category. These businesses are extremely valuable and play a critical role in redirecting economic resources to their most productive uses. Even these businesses have communities they serve. When they become irrationally focused on short-term profit maximization, they can do damage to their communities, which typically comes back to harm them through increased destructive regulations. Some leaders are short-term smart, long-term not-so-smart.

Nonprofit organizations also have constituencies. The Cato Institute is the world's leading libertarian "think tank." In my view, we are owned by our sponsors (contributors) in the same way shareholders own a for-profit business. Cato's board of directors' obligation is to be sure the organization delivers the value we have committed to our sponsors. Obviously, with thousands of sponsors, we cannot do everything every sponsor wants us to do. However, we must clearly outline what our goals are and how those goals are going to be accomplished. Our sponsors then choose to provide support (or not), and we must execute in a highly effective and efficient manner.

At Cato, our client base is extremely broad. In some ways our most important clients are our sponsors. We want to be sure they have the information and insights to understand public policy issues from a libertarian perspective. We are also trying to educate the broader community in the United States and around the world on the libertarian public policies, which are the foundation of a free and prosperous society. Because we have limited resources, some of our most important clients are public opinion leaders across the political spectrum (liberals/progressives, independents, conservatives, libertarians) and across the cultural spectrum (media, politicians, business leaders, and the academy). We want to reinforce the knowledge and understanding of those who share our vision of freedom and to change the minds of those who do not share this vision. The most effective way to achieve this goal is to influence the influencers.

Being very clear about the purpose of the organization is critical to that organization's success. Communicating this purpose with clarity to all major constituencies is essential for excellence. It is particularly important that the employees understand the purpose in a way that is both self-actualizing and self-correcting. Employees who truly understand the purpose of the organization and are vested in the accomplishment of the purpose require far less management.

My dad worked for the Long Lines division of the American Telephone & Telegraph Company (AT&T) before it was broken up. He told me something that still impresses me. At the time, from the late 1950s to the early 1960s, he was a first-line supervisor responsible for maintaining the long-distance telephone lines, which were on telephone poles and subject to weather disruptions. He said he was authorized to incur any cost in order to restore phone service without asking anyone else. In practical terms, there was probably a limit on this authority, but he felt tremendously empowered and completely responsible. If you are a baby boomer like me, you may remember using your phone to call the power company when your power went out. There are some technical reasons why this happens, but a major reason was that AT&T had chosen to give practically complete authority to its first-line supervisors to take care of the customer. This is a lesson we tried to incorporate at BB&T. The closer to the customer the ultimate decision maker is, the better service the customer receives, provided the decision maker has the competence to make the decision. Excellent training should be offered to provide that competence.

Organizations of any size are typically divided into departments, divisions, regions, and the like. It is the responsibility of the leader of that organizational unit to understand and communicate how the department contributes to the success of the overall organization. Departments have customers, which are often internal. They should identify the needs of these internal customers in the context of the "ultimate" customer of the organization. If the members of a team understand who their customers are and how their work impacts the organization's ultimate customers, fellow employees, communities, and shareholders, they will be far more likely to accomplish their task effectively and be much more satisfied with their work. At BB&T, tellers are in the economic success and financial security business; they do not just cash checks.

Other excellent examples are employees at Whole Foods, Starbucks, and Southwest Airlines, who understand that the value proposition is not just the product but rather the employees themselves in many intangible ways. This makes them enjoy their work more, and they do it better.

Let's return to the issue of individual purpose, your purpose. When talking with students, I am often asked how one should decide on a purpose. I do not fully know the answer to that question. However, here are a few thoughts. You are more likely to enjoy something you do relatively well. Thus, a purpose consistent with your strengths is more likely to be fulfilling. I enjoy music; however, I have no musical ability of any kind. Trying to be a musician would not have been a fulfilling experience for me. Many people seem to pursue careers defined by their parents or are trying to prove something (instead of accomplish something) through their career choices.

Most people are more satisfied with their work when it is at the level of their mental abilities. This will surprise you, but one-half of the population is below average (below the mean) in IQ. One-half of the population is below average in critical reasoning. Also, one-half of the population is below average in empathy and other social characteristics. In fact, one-half of the population is below average (and one-half above average) in everything. Also, people think differently. Some people think in big chunks/strategically. Some people see details. And the list goes on. In deciding on a career (or considering a job change), objectively reflect on your strengths and weaknesses. Then reflect on the attributes that are needed in different types of work.

A bank teller does not need to be an intellectual genius. However, she needs to be both detail oriented and empathetic.

My own story may be an indicator of an effective but trial-and-error (or lucky) career search. No one in my direct line of descent had ever graduated from college, but they believed a college education was important. My family moved to Chapel Hill, North Carolina, where the University of North Carolina (UNC) is located, when I was in the eleventh grade. At that time there was a special low tuition rate at UNC for students from Chapel Hill High School and you could live at home, which further reduced the cost. When I was ready to go to college, my dad said he would help pay for my tuition at UNC or I could go to any college I wanted to but I would need to pay myself. I decided to go to UNC.

In those days the massive baby boom population was beginning to hit the universities. At UNC the first day of registration you were supposed to declare a major. So we stood in a long line in hot weather waiting our turn to register. When I got my chance, I said I wanted to be an engineer. Actually, I had no idea what engineers did, but my high school guidance counselor told me because of my math abilities and the Cooter Preference Test results I should be an engineer, and my dad worked with a number of engineers at AT&T. Unfortunately, the registrar said that UNC did not offer engineering—oh! So I asked what they did offer. She started down the alphabetical list, and it being a hot day, I was ready to get this exercise over with. Because all the adults in my family worked in a business, when she got to business administration I told her I would take that one, even though I did not know what a business administrator did. Very scientific.

I graduated from UNC in January. I had applied and been accepted to several law schools, which did not start until the fall. I took a job at BB&T, expecting to go back to law school. However, when I started working at BB&T I really enjoyed banking and saw what attorneys were doing—which did not appeal to me. I subsequently went to MBA school, instead of law school, while I was working.

What is interesting is why I applied to get a job at a bank at all. Nobody in my family had ever been a banker, lawyer, doctor, or any other professional. However, I took a finance course my senior year in college under Avery B. Cohen. He was one of those tough, old, grizzled, no-nonsense, no-bull professors. The course was rigorous and demanding. I certainly did not realize it at the time, but finance uses the same type of mathematical critical thinking skills as engineering. Also, while I certainly would not have said so at the time, the rigor and no nonsense really appealed to me. The reason I applied for a job at a bank was because of Avery B. Cohen. Interestingly, my first cousin, who was living with my family (to save money), took the course with me. He also became a bank executive. Talk about making the world a better place to live! Interestingly, at the time we made fun of Avery B. Cohen, but he was the professor who inspired me the most to find my purpose. And I cannot remember the names of a single one of the cushy professors who did not push me.

I am convinced that if I had gone to engineering school, I would subsequently have gotten an MBA and run a manufacturing business instead of a bank. If I had gone to law school, I would have become a corporate attorney and ultimately managed a business. In other words, even though "luck" was involved, my talents pulled me in a certain direction, and while the concrete outcome easily could have been different, the general context of a type of career flowed naturally from my abilities.

Another question students ask that relates to purpose is whether when I went to work for BB&T my intention was to become CEO and make a lot of money. I liked being CEO and I certainly liked making a lot of money, but my goal was never to be CEO or to make a lot of money. My goal was always to do whatever job I had better than anyone had ever done it and to understand how the job related to the rest of the organization. This focus created a short-term empowering purpose. In striving for mastery, I was forcing myself to learn, and I was having a good time. Also, when you do a job extremely well, the odds of getting a promotion increase significantly. In addition people like to be around individuals who are focused and committed to excellence in their work. When an individual is focused on a promotion instead of excellence, it can be offensive to some members of the team.

In searching for a personal sense of purpose, reflect objectively on your strengths and weaknesses and the skill set that is appropriate for various careers. You may want to talk to successful practitioners to see what they believe are the attributes for success in that endeavor.

It is extremely important that you consider careers beyond those dependent on college-based skills. If you have mechanical skills, you may be more talented at work using these skills instead of the type of work for which college is designed. One of the tragedies of our time is the number of people who have outstanding mechanical aptitudes but work dissatisfied in job structures that do not use these attributes.

In a certain context, neither organizations nor societies have a vision or a purpose. Vision and purpose are attributes of individuals. However, successful leaders create shared visions and purposes where the members of the organization are moving together toward a common vision and purpose.

The vision of the Founding Fathers as expressed in the Declaration of Independence is a free society where all individuals are equal before the law and where each individual has the fundamental right to his or her own life, to liberty, and to the pursuit of personal happiness. This shared vision has created a unique American sense of life.

In the context of this vision, the purpose of government as seen by the Founding Fathers was to protect each individual's rights, including the right to the product of his or her labor.

Individuals need a clear sense of purpose to be successful and happy. Organizations and societies that can energize a shared vision and sense of purpose among their participants will be dramatically more successful in the long term.

Values in the Pursuit of Happiness

3

Reality Grounded

THERE SEEMS TO BE AN ENDLESS STREAM OF ETHICAL DEVIATIONS IN society today. Yet many people realize that having a clear set of values to guide their lives is important. However, few use their values very effectively. Most people have a hodgepodge of values that they have arrived at somewhat randomly throughout their lives. They do one thing, and then feel guilty because they did not do something differently. Individuals often hold conflicting values that are inconsistent with real-world living.

Very few individuals have asked themselves the fundamental question: What is the purpose of values? They provide us with principles that, if we live by them, improve the probability of staying alive, being successful, and ultimately being happy. So a proper set of values is about achieving success and happiness.

Even having the right values does not guarantee success and happiness, because things happen in Mother Nature beyond our control. However, having the right values improves the probability of success and happiness.

If you grasp values in this context, it is clear that they are not arbitrary. They do not fall from the sky, nor are they necessarily what your mom, dad, Sunday school teacher, or kindergarten teacher told you when you were five years old. Establishing a value system that promotes your life, your success, and your happiness is a scientific problem. The fundamental question to answer is: Given the laws of nature, Mother Nature, and given human nature, what principles are likely to lead to your success and happiness?

Over the next few chapters we will discuss the 10 core values that were the foundation for BB&T's success. These are my personal values. I believe that these principles are applicable to all individuals, all organizations, and society as a whole. Make your own judgment.

As we discuss these values, you will note that they are both non-contradictory and integrated. Fail on one of the values and fail on all the others. I also believe they are comprehensive, which will be discussed in Chapter 12. Before we talk about these values, it's important to have a firm understanding of the nature of reality and how it impacts our ability to lead and make decisions. The next few chapters explore this concept.

Reality Grounded

What is, is. This is one of the most fundamental philosophical observations of all times. Reality is irrefutable. It is what it is. We do not get to vote on reality. A baby is born this morning at your local hospital. Mom, dad, the doctors, nurses, trees, and all of nature are already here. The baby does not get to make it up. In fact, the baby's task in life is to use her abilities to stay alive, become successful, and ultimately be happy. At some point you were that baby and you have been trying to stay alive, be successful, and be happy, given the facts of reality.

Successful businesses rely on fact-based decision making. There is a subtle difference between facts and reality. It may be that your competition has a superior product today. You cannot change that fact. However, you can develop a process to make a product better than your competitors in the future.

The law of gravity is a fundamental reality and is immutable. The existence of the law of gravity does not mean humans cannot build an airplane, but the airplane must be consistent with the law of reality. As Francis Bacon explained, "Nature to be mastered, must first be obeyed."

At one level, the existence of reality is self-evident. And yet the vast majority of people are in resistance to reality, which is an unhealthy place to be. People make three major mistakes in regard to reality. These are actually epistemological mistakes (errors in thinking), but they relate to reality. These mistakes have a significant impact on the life of an individual and the quality of life on the planet.

"Wishing something is so does not make it so" is a metaphor for the ultimate psychological sin of evasion. Evasion occurs when you are presented with some piece of information that you know should be examined, but you refuse to examine it because the information threatens something you want to believe about yourself or you want to believe about the world. Oftentimes, you simply cannot bear to hear the news. This means you are detached from reality, which is a very unhealthy place to be.

I started my career as a small business lender. One of the primary reasons small businesses fail is the leader of that business evades. The business is going along well, then something negative happens in the economy or at home and the owner of the business does not want to hear it and she runs the business into the ground. If you cannot face a problem, you cannot fix it.

A more dramatic example is Citigroup in the financial crisis of 2007–2009. At the time, Citigroup was the largest financial institution in the world. People at Citigroup hired a group of geniuses, PhDs from Harvard, MIT, and so on, to run their affordable housing (subprime lending) business. I guarantee that before any of us knew there were problems in the subprime housing market, the geniuses in the backroom of Citigroup saw the problem. What did they do? They evaded. Why did they evade? Because if they surfaced the problem they would make a lot less money and Citigroup would make a lot less money in the short term. So they ran Citigroup right into serious financial troubles.

Unfortunately, many of us evade in some aspect of our lives. Your parents, friends, spouse, and manager all have been telling you about your evasions. The next time you hear something from someone you trust about some aspect of your behavior or about the nature of the world that you have heard before but have not wanted to consider, think about it. Being detached from reality is an unhealthy place to be.

The second major error in regard to reality is the belief in popularity. Reality is independent from popularity. In 1600, the vast majority of the population was certain the sun went around the earth. The sun comes up in the east and goes down in the west. Besides, if the earth is going around the sun, why don't we fly off? In 1632, Galileo proved that the earth went around the sun. That the vast majority of the population thought the sun went around the earth had no effect on the sun or the earth.

A more recent example relates to subprime lending. Given its size, it is understandable why Citigroup got in the subprime lending business, but a number of banks BB&T's size also became involved in this high-risk business. When I asked the CEOs of firms why they got into this subprime lending business, they all had a song and dance, but in the end they all said, "Everybody else was doing it."

Have you ever gone along with a group because you did not want to challenge what everybody else wanted to do? Have you sometimes been sorry? Entrepreneurs almost always go against the crowd. They see opportunities in a different light than the group. They explore the world from a reality-grounded view. And reality is independent of popularity. Great damage has been done and millions of lives lost because too few individuals have had the courage to challenge the crowd. Groupthink can be very dangerous in organizations and in society.

The third error is the most difficult to see. Reality is independent of authority. Just because an authority says it is so does not make it so. In 1632, Galileo publishes his book and proves the earth goes around the sun. The pope reads Galileo's book. The pope is the spiritual and intellectual leader of Western civilization. He is a highly educated and intellectual person. He does not like Galileo's book because it challenges some of his fundamental beliefs. He puts Galileo under house arrest for the rest of his life and bans Galileo's book. Fortunately, a few copies of the book leak out and lead to Newton's discoveries and the Industrial Revolution. Whether the pope liked it or not, the earth kept going around the sun. Reality is independent of authority.

A more current example is errors made by Standard & Poor's (S&P), Moody's, and Fitch in the financial crisis of 2007–2009. These firms were the authorities in rating financial instruments.

They had a special government-created oligopoly in rating financial products. They were examined by the Securities and Exchange Commission (SEC) and were supposed to be the experts, the authorities, on rating financial instruments.

Unfortunately, they did a poor job. They rated many financial instruments A+ when they were F−. These inaccurate ratings contributed to trillions of dollars of losses and cost millions of jobs. You can be pretty unhappy about these poor ratings.

Relying on these ratings was an avoidable mistake. Ultimately, the responsibility for accepting the ratings is on the purchasers of bonds who blindly used these ratings. One reason BB&T did better than many of our competitors during the financial crisis is that we did not buy financial instruments based solely on S&P's, Moody's, and Fitch's ratings. Some of us had been through the real estate–based economic correction of the early 1990s and when studying these financial instruments realized that the rating agencies were far too optimistic about the losses that would occur if/when we had another economic correction.

While we do have to rely to some degree on authorities, we are responsible for evaluating our authorities especially in fields where we have some knowledge. The buyers of the rated bonds were sophisticated investors and should have known better than to purchase these instruments without independent examination. If you have a serious medical issue, it may be worthwhile to get a second opinion. If an authority arrives at a conclusion inconsistent with reality, the authority is wrong, not reality.

One of the most important aspects of reality is the law of cause and effect or the law of causality. You can visualize the law of causality by picturing one billiard ball hitting another billiard ball. However, the law of causality is far deeper than this picture. The law of causality says that everything in nature has a nature and everything in nature must act consistently with its nature. Billiard balls must act like billiard balls. Elephants must act like elephants. And as human beings we have a nature and we must act consistent with our nature.

Humans are not billiard balls. We are not deterministic. One of the most important aspects of our nature is that we have free will. We must make choices. We have to decide. The self-evidence of free will is a set of decisions you have been making since you were very young, which you make every few seconds, and which only you can make. Those choices are to focus your mind or not. To be here or not. While you are reading this book (or especially when you are listening to a lecture), you may choose to go in and out of focus. No one can stay in focus all of the time, but you choose whether to be in focus or not. In reading this book, I will possibly raise an issue or draw an implication you do not want to hear. You may choose to go out of focus at that point. One way people evade is to go out of focus.

In all aspects of your individual life and in an organizational context, the most important foundation for any decision is the facts. Wishing, popularity, and authority cannot change reality. In my 40-year career many of the most destructive decisions I have seen made were based on some form of evasion.

Do our political leaders make decisions based on reality? Or are they like the pope in the Galileo story? Being president does not give you the ability to wish away reality. One of the most important questions you should ask yourself in choosing the best political candidate is whether that candidate is willing to face the facts. Or does he offer platitudes and bromides, accompanied by easy and painless solutions that sound good but are not grounded in reality? What is, is.

4

Reason (Objectivity)

THE OTHER UNIQUE ASPECT OF HUMANKIND'S NATURE IS THAT WE have the capacity to reason objectively based on the facts of reality. Everything that is alive has some method of staying alive. A lion can hunt. A deer has speed to run from the hunters. Humans have the capacity to think. Our ability to think is literally our only means of survival, success, and happiness. There are no shortcuts, no free lunches.

We are extremely fortunate that one of the great geniuses of history, Aristotle, taught us how to think in 300 BC. He said that we should begin with premises based on the facts and then use induction and deduction to derive conclusions. Those conclusions have to be integrated without contradiction. The fundamental rule of logic is to avoid contradiction. The conclusion then can become a premise for the next step in the thinking process.

It is interesting how we try to improve our thinking. We typically focus on higher levels of thinking. I taught in a graduate business school, so I certainly see value in this type of effort. However, the real lever in thinking is your premises. If you have an error in your premises, you will of necessity have an error in your conclusion. If you build a 20-story building on quicksand, it will fall over. On college campuses you can encounter professors who have the type of linear intelligence that is required for a PhD. However, their arguments are based on premises inconsistent with reality, and they cannot hold the broader context. So while they appear intelligent, their conclusions, especially outside their very specific field, are often irrational.

It is interesting to reflect on the source of your most important premises, your most fundamental beliefs—beliefs that have a profound impact on the quality of your life. Where did you get your most fundamental premises, your most basic beliefs? Largely, from your mom, dad, Sunday school teacher, and kindergarten teacher when you were young. Where did they get their fundamental beliefs? From their moms, dads, and Sunday school teachers when they were young. Where did they get their fundamental beliefs? From their moms, dads, and Sunday school teachers when they were young, and so on.

What are the implications of this method of developing your most important, most fundamental beliefs? First, many of your beliefs are primitive. They have been passed on from one generation to another often without examination. Secondly, there is a high probability your basic beliefs are a hodgepodge. Some make sense; some do not, hence the contradictions. Would you be comfortable if your doctor performed medical treatment based on ideas passed down from one generation to the next? Is your fundamental method of thinking based on primitive beliefs? Would you let your doctor treat you based on primitive beliefs?

Even if you love your parents, you can probably see aspects of their behavior and thinking that keep them from being as successful and, more important, as happy as they could be. You may have a different content, but the odds are very high that you have the same context. The most important action you can take to improve your thinking ability and increase the probability of being happy is to objectively examine your basic beliefs as an adult. Reject all premises that are inconsistent with reality; they cannot be so. Also reject all contradictions, because contradictions cannot exist in reality. Incorrect premises drive destructive conclusions.

Deduction is the concrete application of a general principle. For example: "All humans are mortal. Socrates is human, therefore Socrates is mortal." The concrete application of general principles is a very important human ability. The good news is that if you are reading this book, you are almost certainly effective at deduction. Unfortunately, many people cannot deduce correctly, including a disproportionate number of politicians. The rules for deduction are long established. In fact the most common reason for deductive mistakes is evasion. The deductive thinker does not want to hear the conclusion that appropriately follows, so he evades.

As useful as deduction is, the real power in thinking is induction. Induction occurs when we are able to draw a general conclusion from a series of concrete examples. How did we decide that all humans are mortal?

The basic expression of induction is concept formation. All humans can form concepts, some individuals are better at concept formation than others. When you were young, you saw that chairs were like each other and different than other things. You applied the word/concept *chair* to concrete things in the real world. When you made this association, your parents got very excited, because they realized that this was the beginning of the thinking process. If you have children, you have gone through the same experience—from the parental perspective. Next you saw that tables were like each other and different than other things, and you developed a word/concept *table*. At some point you made a significant intellectual leap. You grasped that even though table and chairs did not look like each other, they shared a similar role, and you grasped the word/concept *furniture*. As you progressed, you were able to grasp more and more complex concepts using the same mental integration fundamentally based on seeing how things and ideas were alike and different from other things and ideas.

Several thoughts about concept formation: First, concepts are incredibly powerful tools for thinking. For example, there are billions of individual chairs in the world. In one concept, you have been able to grasp billions of separate entities. If you had to think of chairs perceptually instead of conceptually, all you could think about would be chairs. Of course, if humans thought that way, we could not have invented chairs.

A second important thought is that understanding concept formation can enable you to vanquish those skeptics who claim you cannot know anything with certainty and yet you can simultaneously reinforce that there is always more to be learned. Take the simple concept—chair. As an adult you know much more about chairs than when you were a child. However, if your initial understanding of chairs was correct, your knowledge of chairs was certain, but it was incomplete. You cannot know everything about anything until you know everything about everything because everything in the universe is related (not relative, but related). But just because you do not know everything possible about chairs does not mean that what you know about chairs is somehow incorrect or inadequate. Such a standard would be completely irrational given humans' means of knowledge.

However, we can always learn more about anything. You will learn more about chairs as you move through life. The rule is to keep all of your concepts open for additional information, but this does not mean you cannot be certain about what you do know.

One additional thought about concept formation. Concepts are fundamentally hierarchical. They build on each other. You have to grasp the concepts of chair and table before you can grasp the concept of furniture and so on. Higher-level concepts are dependent on lower-level concepts. In forming concepts, you started with chairs and worked your way up to very complex ideas like freedom, justice, love, the role of government, economic systems, and so forth. The good news is you did an excellent job with concepts like chair and furniture. The bad news is that it is likely that you cheated on upper-level concepts. You almost certainly developed your upper-level concepts from authorities. This does not mean the concepts are invalid, but you need to be certain that you fully grasp these concepts before you try to claim knowledge. Even the most complex concepts must be traceable back to reality or they are not valid.

Why talk about concept formation in a book about leadership and the pursuit of happiness? Because concepts are the tools we use to think effectively. Well-integrated concepts are necessary to achieve mastery in any field of endeavor. You are competing in a new world. There are over 7 billion people on this planet. Many are better educated then they used to be. All are much closer due to technology, and most are willing to work a lot harder than you for a lot less. If you are to be successful in this new competitive world, you need to become a master of your field of endeavor. To achieve mastery requires developing integrated concepts that can become decision tools for the application of deductive reasoning.

We have all encountered individuals who have achieved mastery in their field of endeavor—and many more people who have not achieved mastery. In Chapter 2, I shared the story of Avery B. Cohen, who was a master teacher. Unfortunately, some of the teachers I encountered in my education were just marking time.

Probably all of us have experienced doctors who did not create a sense of confidence and/or seemed to be focused on something besides our health. On the other hand, my current family physician is clearly a master who has significantly contributed to my physical well-being.

In the banking business, I knew a number of master lenders who could analyze complex financial information and make extremely consistent integrated decisions. Their decisions radically outperformed financial models. All the risk management models in the world cannot make individual bad loans into a good loan portfolio. On the other hand, if the individual loans are good, the loan portfolio will be good, no matter whether it is mathematically modeled or not. (Someone, please tell that to the Federal Reserve!)

There are master plumbers, electricians, beauticians, car mechanics, homemakers, and so on. Mastery matters because it is the foundation for both success and the sense of achievement on which real happiness is based. Also masters in any field make the world a better place to live for the rest of us.

What is required to achieve mastery? Comprehensively answering this question is beyond the scope of this book, but I do want to plant a few seeds. Selecting a career for which you have some natural talents is an important starting point. It is difficult but not impossible to become a master in a vocation for which you do not have some natural ability. This is why encouraging students to attend college can be destructive if their primary natural abilities are mechanical aptitudes. In addition, individuals who achieve mastery tend to read and study more, depending on the nature of the field of endeavor. They also take advantage of many types of educational seminars.

However, the most distinguishing characteristic of masters is the ability to learn from life experiences. In fact, as human beings we are primarily life experience learners. Masters use a combination of the broad principles that can come from formal education and both modify and apply those principles based on their life experiences.

The result is that masters develop concepts that enable them to integrate more complex data and make better decisions. They can often "see" solutions based on subconscious integration of the concepts they have grasped from other experiences, that is, from inductions. You can significantly improve your ability to create concepts by consciously realizing that concepts are the tools of thinking and that you can integrate them by looking for similarities and differences. Put the similar things together.

Individuals who achieve mastery also do two simple but profound things unusually effectively. Probably all of us can associate with learning from mistakes. You have probably made mistakes that caused you to change your life for the better. On the other hand, many times we do not learn from our mistakes. Sometimes we do something that we wish we had not done but simultaneously realize we have done the same thing before, possibly multiple times. Occasionally, we embed these mistakes into our personality and have the opportunity to make the same mistake over and over again.

Why do we not always learn from our mistakes? In order to learn from your mistake, you first have to admit it is a mistake, but you also have to identify the real cause of the mistake, not the surface cause. Sometimes we refuse to admit we made a mistake. Equally important, when we do admit to making a mistake, we do not want to face the real cause (because this realization is psychologically painful), so we offer a superficial explanation of the cause of the mistake to ourselves. In other words, we evade. And when we evade, we are detached from reality and cannot learn or grow. Before Bear Stearns failed, the leadership of the company evaded the reputational risk in its off balance sheet subprime bond portfolio. However, the market called their evasion.

Superior experiential learners evade less and therefore learn more rapidly than others. Because they take full responsibility for their mistakes, they can move on and avoid the same mistakes in the future.

Superior experiential learners also live their lives in focus. Unfortunately, most people live most of their lives out of focus—brain on idle. When you are out of focus, you cannot learn. When I was CEO of BB&T, we operated with 33 community banks. I visited each of the banks periodically and had the pleasure of having lunch with our local advisory board members who were business and community leaders. I never had a boring lunch. These individuals were always asking questions, expressing opinions, engaged, challenging, discussing, in gear. It was easy to see why they were successful. They were paying attention to life.

In my career at BB&T, I observed a number of high school graduates who joined the bank in entry-level jobs who subsequently outperformed their college graduate contemporaries. These individuals consistently demonstrated an objectivity about themselves and others that allowed them to learn more rapidly from their experiences. They were willing to take reasonable risk and to learn, and they evaded far less when they made mistakes. In addition, it was clear they were more focused on their work. They paid attention to details and were constantly striving to get better. They also aggressively took advantage of any educational opportunities the bank offered.

While having a high IQ may (or may not) be an advantage, the most successful people I know evade less and stay in focus more, which is a huge competitive advantage in life.

When I discuss reason, sometimes individuals ask me about the role of faith. Frankly, I try not to discuss faith or religion, because I am not an expert and there is often an emotional reaction to this issue. My own view, for whatever it is worth, is that when God created the universe, He created it exactly as he wanted it—Mother Nature (the laws of nature) is exactly as God desired. When God created humankind, He created humans exactly how He wanted them to be. Human nature is exactly as it should be. After all, God is omniscient and omnipotent.

In this context, God gave humankind a very specific means of survival—our capacity to reason. This tool provides us with the means to understand His laws of nature. The evidence for a good life is available to us using the tools God gave us. So whether evolution or God's wisdom gave us the capacity to reason is irrelevant. Reason is our means of survival, success, and happiness. This is one man's opinion, for whatever it is worth.

It follows from the facts that an individual's ability to think is her means of success and that organizations are simply groups of individuals. An organization that encourages thinking will be more successful in the long term. Obviously, certain types of work require more thinking than other types.

The assembly line clearly increased productivity. However, I suspect the Taylor method of reducing tasks to extreme simplicity probably reduced instead of increased productivity. The numerous other advances in technology that were occurring at the same time offset the Taylor method mistake. In my opinion, much of the union movement was not about higher wages, but about the degradation of the meaningfulness of work. Those organizations that find ways to use the thinking abilities of their employees will be more successful in the long term.

At the societal level, if one accepts reason as a value, the fundamental role of an educational system becomes self-evident: to teach students to think critically, to think logically, and thereby to reason objectively based on the facts of reality. The test of an educational system is its ability to educate students to be critical thinkers and thereby to be able to make rational decisions. If individuals can think rationally, the vast majority of the so-called socialization issue disappears. It is irrational thinking that creates the socialization problems.

Unfortunately, by any objective measure against this standard, the government-owned school system has failed miserably. The United States has drastically increased investment on a per-student basis, and yet critical thinking skills have not increased. (See Cato Institute's website: http://www.cato.org/edspending.) Obviously, there is a problem with the system design. The most fundamental design problem with the government-owned schools is that their purpose is not to teach students to be critical thinkers but rather to socialize them. And the system cannot learn from mistakes, because there is no incentive to learn from mistakes. If reason is a fundamental value, the long-term consequences of a failed education system to our society are tremendous. In a rapidly changing, highly competitive, globally integrated environment, by the time one learns a technical skill it is likely to be outdated. You are chasing a moving target. The skill that matters is the ability to think critically. As computers take over more routine tasks, critical thinking becomes ever more important. One of the primary reasons the middle class is declining economically in the United States is because even our so-called good government schools are failing to provide the students with the critical thinking skills that are essential for success in today's world. This topic will be discussed further in Chapter 6.

5

Independent Thinking
(Responsibility/Creativity)

INDEPENDENT THINKING MEANS MAKING DECISIONS AND judgments for yourself using your personal ability to reason from the facts of reality. Independence is the realization that you are responsible for your own judgments. We learn a great deal from other people. Teamwork is very important, as will be discussed. But each of us thinks alone. No one can think for you.

One of the reasons independent thinking is critical is that it makes two important attributes both possible and necessary: responsibility and creativity.

The most important meta-psychological decision you can make is to choose to be responsible for yourself. If you view yourself as a victim in any respect of your life, you are giving your power away. If you are a victim, someone else has to change to make you happy, and you cannot change anyone else.

People can view themselves as victims because of their race, sex, nationality, religion, and so forth. The most common reason people view themselves as victims is because of their mothers: "If my mother had only . . . [fill in the blank]." This mother victimology is the primary revenue source for psychologists and psychiatrists. It is a major revenue stream for the pharmaceutical industry. Can mothers ever do their job right?

Give your mother a break. Some mothers may be more caring, thoughtful, and loving than others, but you are responsible for you. It is true that bad things happen to good people and good things happen to bad people. Mother Nature just is. However, you are responsible for doing the best you can with what happens to you.

Something very important most people know, but do not want to admit, is: we are all alone. At least at the level of consciousness we are all alone—sorry. Therefore, only you can be responsible for you. It is not possible for anyone else to be responsible for you. In the end, you control you. The other side of this concept is also true. You cannot be responsible for anyone else. This leads to a classic parental error and a classic managerial error.

You cannot be responsible for your children. If you try to be responsible for your children, you will set them up to fail. However, you are responsible to teach your children to be responsible for themselves. (It is best to start by being sure the child recognizes the appropriate negative and positive consequences for his or her actions; consequences matter.)

In a managerial role, you cannot be responsible for your employees. If you try to be responsible for your employees, you will set them and yourself up to fail. You are responsible to teach your employees to be responsible for themselves. If you have employees who refuse to become personally responsible, replace them. Lack of responsibility is unacceptable in an organizational context.

I believe the single most important issue in our society today is personal responsibility. A free society is fundamentally dependent on personal responsibility. A question I ask student groups is: "Are you responsible for yourself, or are you entitled to what someone else produces?" If you choose not to be personally responsible, then you have chosen to be dependent. Furthermore, you cannot be entitled to be happy. Happiness has to be earned. Societal systems that encourage dependency destroy the capacity of individuals to achieve genuine happiness. The choice to be dependent is the choice not to be happy.

Creativity/innovation is by definition the source of all human progress. Unless someone creates something that is better, there cannot be any progress. Anything that is better is different. Creativity/innovation is only possible to an independent thinker. Someone who thinks like the crowd cannot be creative and cannot be innovative. Although that person may be quite productive in a maintenance sense, he or she cannot genuinely contribute to human progress.

At the individual level there are many obstacles to creativity. One obstacle is our education system. Several studies have shown that at five years of age, the vast majority of children rate highly on creativity. We have all seen the creativity of kindergarteners in their art. By 25 years of age, practically none of these same students are creative. Our school system teaches us how not to be creative. Being creative is sorely punished in most schools. Teachers are not selected or awarded for their creativity. By the way, the Chinese education system has this problem in spades, and this is an important limit on raising their standard of living beyond a certain level. The Chinese are fundamentally dependent on U.S. innovation.

Many people have come to believe that creativity is some magical, unexplainable attribute. In fact, creativity is an intellectual process. It is true that most of our creativity takes place in the subconscious, but most of our thinking also takes place in the subconscious. The following is not a perfect analogy, but it is a useful one. Think of yourself (your conscious mind) as a computer programmer and your brain as the computer. Since you were very young, you have been "writing" computer programs that you push down into your subconscious. You spend much of your life "operating" on these programs without ever being aware that the programs are driving your behavior. However, you wrote the programs, and you can change them if you desire. Changing the programs is a difficult process, but it is doable.

Most creativity takes place in the subconscious on programs you have written or are writing. Your conscious mind can direct that activity, but part of the activity is on autopilot. Sometimes the creative revelations "pop" into your conscious mind from the subconscious. But there is nothing magical or mystical about creativity. It is an intellectual activity.

Studies of creative adults indicate that they have at least two common characteristics. First, creative people think they are capable of being creative. Most people believe they are not capable of being creative, which can prevent them from being creative. And secondly, creative individuals believe they should be creative.

At the organizational level, sustaining creativity is a balancing act. Organizations must have an agreed-upon set of fundamental principles that direct behavior in the organization. Furthermore, organizations typically have an embedded set of processes that are necessary for consistency of performance. How do you allow for creativity in organizations in this context?

Let me share with you some of the things we did at BB&T to accomplish this objective. First, we operated a highly decentralized organization with decision making close to the customer. We invested heavily in training to provide the context that allowed the decentralization to work. BB&T's university has courses on "productive creativity." By productive creativity, I mean changes that improve overall organizational performance. Many creative changes (perhaps 90 percent) do not improve overall organizational performance. Some creative changes positively impact a department at the expense of the rest of the organization. In this context, these "creative" changes are actually destructive. Within the context of the productive creativity program, all managers had innovation goals on which they were measured. The cultural context was that the only thing not subject to change was our vision, mission, and values. Everything else was open to improvement.

As indicated, at the societal level, creativity/innovation is the source of all (100 percent) of human progress. This is why entrepreneurs are so important. Entrepreneurs take the ideas of engineers, scientists, and academics and turn their ideas into reality. Without entrepreneurship, there is no progress.

In order for individuals to be creative, to innovate, they must be able to pursue their truth. If you are forced to act like 2 plus 2 is 5, you literally cannot think. Many government rules and regulations force individuals to act as if 2 plus 2 is 5. Government rules and regulations destroy innovation and creativity. We need a fundamental rule of law for economic success as it provides a framework for mutually beneficial relationships; however, the massive regulatory state of today is the enemy of economic progress.

Entrepreneurs are basically experimenters. Most entrepreneurial ideas, like most creative ideas, are bad. A few are good. A very few are tremendously beneficial. Free markets answer the question whether an idea is good or bad based on the reaction of the consumers of the product or service that is being created.

Statism of all types (socialism, communism, fascism) is doomed to failure because these systems destroy innovation and creativity. List the innovative accomplishments of the Soviet Union. It is a very, very short list. The biggest enemy of innovation is the use of force, and the government is the initiator of force by definition. If you do not believe me, try not paying your taxes.

The Cato Institute recently published the book *Poverty and Progress* by Deepak Lal, which looks at human well-being since *Homo sapiens* evolved. From the evolution of *Homo sapiens* until the late 1700s, although some progress had been made, human life expectancy remained essentially unchanged at about 25 to 30 years. In the late 1700s, something happened that started the transformation of human life expectancy on the planet. This fuse was first lit in Western civilization and is now taking the rest of the planet by storm. There was an invention in the late 1700s that was more important than fire or the wheel. This revolutionary invention was a combination of the rule of law and individual rights, both economic and political, which is capitalism. Capitalism allowed individuals to think for themselves, to experiment with new ideas, products, and services. Freedom led to economic well-being.

Over the last 20 years, the rate of extreme poverty in the world has halved. A number of scholars, including those at the Brookings Institution, have stated that such a dramatic reduction in extreme poverty is unprecedented in human history. It is telling that increased prosperity coincides with the spread of economic freedom in general and free trade in particular. (See Cato's website: http://www.HumanProgress.org.)

By the way, the author of *Poverty and Progress* concludes that the greatest threat to eliminating poverty on the planet is the environmental movement. Much economic progress has been based on industries using energy. Ironically, the environmentally correct progressive/liberal elites cause the most harm to the poverty stricken of the world.

While we learn a great deal from other people, and teamwork is critically important to many complex endeavors, only individuals think. Groups do not think. In order to be productive, individuals must be free to think for themselves, to pursue their truths as they know them. Free societies demand personal responsibility and make creativity possible. Thinking individuals who are innovative, creative, and personally responsible make human flourishing possible.

6

Productivity (Profitability)

Productivity is about getting the task accomplished. It is about action in reality that produces a desired outcome. Productivity includes the creation of physical goods. Growing corn and building automobiles are productive activities. Writing a book, giving a speech, or developing a computer program are also productive activities. The creation of ideas and the transmission of those ideas into useful reality can be very productive.

At the individual level, productivity is typically driven by a fundamental psychological commitment to get the job done. There is a basic psychological difference between high performance and nonperformance in regard to productivity. High performers have a gut-level commitment to complete the task, while nonperformers are often looking for an excuse to fail.

Let me concretize this concept with a story from BB&T. When I was CEO of BB&T, I would visit many of our branches and home office departments. When I would visit a branch where the results were not satisfactory, the branch manager would inevitably have a story. The story would be that rates of loans the competitor bank was charging were too low, so the BB&T branch manager could not develop any loan business. And the rates the competitor bank was paying for certificates of deposit were too high. So BB&T's

branch manager could not attract any deposits. And the stoplight across the street made it difficult for customers to get into the office. And the home office was not managing the computer system well, which was why the clients were unhappy. And so forth. Sometimes there was truth about the impact of these obstacles. There may be obstacles that simply cannot be overcome. Sometimes we replaced the branch manager, and the branch's performance subsequently improved radically.

This experience contrasts with our Sterling Award winners. This was an award program for our most productive client contact employees. Several thousand employees were eligible for the Sterling Award. In the 18 years that I was involved with the Sterling Award program, a few employees won the award for 5 or 10 years in a row but no one won the award every year. However, the same 25 percent of employees consistently were winners. An individual would win the award, not win for a year or two, and then win again, and so on. If you talked to these high performers, they would tell you what they did and how much more they would do the next year. They faced the same obstacles, but they were focused on the end results. They failed, but they came back. They never quit. They had a gut-level commitment to get the job done. Nonperformers often look for the excuses to fail. High performers focus on the end results. In a certain sense, they never fail, because they play the game to win within the rules.

In a broad context, there is a balancing act between planning, thinking, and doing. Productive individuals do plan and think, but they also act. The action can be an intangible such as a speech, but it is an action. There is a tendency by some individuals to overanalyze and procrastinate. Others may act without thinking. To be productive in most responsibilities requires thinking, planning, and acting. In teams, as will be discussed, it is often desirable to include individuals who have a bias to analyze and some with a bias for action. However, the goal is to get the job done, to produce.

At the business organizational level, in a true free market, profit is the desired outcome. Profit is simply the difference between the value of what we produce and the cost of producing it. The bigger the profit (long term), the better. To be highly profitable (long term) a business organization must be very efficient. It must be very productive. Productivity, in the broad context, drives profitability. At BB&T, one of our key performance measures was the efficiency ratio. This is the ratio of expenses to revenue. We were consistently in the top 5 percent of major financial institutions in this measurement. This focus of efficiency/productivity was a significant driver of our strong financial results.

Tragically, profit has become a bad term to many people, including business professors and some business students. One should never apologize for making an honest profit. Apologize for taking a loss. Losses represent destruction of wealth. Profit is the creation of wealth and the source of human well-being. It is critically important in a business organization to defend the concept of justly earned profit. Otherwise, its employees will not be able to morally defend their work, which will undermine their productivity.

Three Pillars of Human Productivity–Human Flourishing

The only true natural resource is the human mind. Three hundred years ago oil was useless to human beings. Oil is useless today to a bear. Someone invented a use for oil. Thirty years ago telecommunications went through thick, expensive cables made of copper. Today telecommunications travel through inexpensive fiber optics (made of silicon, the earth's most common material) or through the air. These inventions of the human mind have made the computer age possible. There is only one true natural resource—the human mind. In this context, there are three "pillars" that are the foundation for human productivity–human flourishing. These pillars enable an individual human being to be productive. Since both organizations and societies are simply groups of human beings, the same pillars are the source of organizational and societal well-being.

As we discuss the societal aspect of these pillars, it is interesting to reflect on the question as to why today we are in the sixth year of the slowest economic recovery in U.S. history. Yet we should be having an economic boom. There are major advances in technology occurring, freer global trade is raising productivity, and the U.S. energy revolution is transformational. Why is the country not growing much more rapidly?

Knowledge

The first pillar is knowledge. In order to be productive you must know how to do something. Knowledge has always been necessary for human survival. Primitive people had to learn how to find berries and how to hunt.

Today knowledge is increasing at an accelerating pace. In addition, the amount of knowledge to simply sustain our standard of living is huge. Furthermore, in today's world the type of know-how required has changed significantly. Although technical knowledge is necessary, it is constantly changing. By the time you learn technical skills, the skills have changed.

The most important type of knowledge to have in the twenty-first century is the know-how to think critically, to reason, and to make objective decisions based on the facts. Critical thinking ability is the defining knowledge/skill in our world.

At the individual level, you need the technical skill to perform your job, but more important is your ability to think critically in an appropriate relation to the complexity of your job responsibilities. You must commit yourself to being a lifelong learner with an active mind.

The ability of an organization to be successful is fundamentally determined by the know-how of its employees and the ability of its leaders to integrate the specialized knowledge of the various members of the organization. The most successful organizations create a culture that supports lifetime learning. Requirements for both individual and organizational know-how have been discussed and will be further concretized in Chapters 17, 18, 20, and 21.

Unfortunately, at the societal level, the objective fact is that the U.S. government-run school system has failed by the critical thinking criteria. This probably, more than any single factor, explains the relative decline of the middle class. Middle-class children typically attend government schools and do not learn the critical thinking skills that are essential in the new competitive global environment. They are having to compete with computers that can replace low-level thinking. The government school system has not responded to this fundamental change in the required skills in this new world.

It is not surprising that government schools have failed. Give me an example of a successful government-run monopoly. How about VA hospitals?

The reason government schools are not successful is that they are immune to the competitive forces of free markets and therefore are not required to innovate. In business, we like to talk about being innovative, but most business leaders do not really want to innovate. But if your firm does not innovate, it will not be able to compete. In addition, if you run your business poorly, it will fail.

If a public high school does a very poor job, however, it will get more resources—witness the Washington, D.C., public school system, which has one of the highest per-pupil costs and worst per-pupil results. Of course, the answer from the government school community is more money.

The solution to the failure of the government school system to produce students with critical thinking skills is to replace it. The answer to education is private, for-profit, unregulated schools. If it is appropriate to subsidize poor children, do so with vouchers and/or tax credits. Do not continue to subsidize failing government schools, which include many schools considered to be successful. They are only successful relative to even less-productive schools.

The method markets use to solve problems is through experimentation. For every Google there were 1,000 failed Google-type companies. For every Walmart there are 1,000 failed Walmart-type companies. The solution to the education problem is thousands of educational experiments. Some will be significantly more successful than others (almost all will be better than the current government school systems). There are the likes of Bill Gates, Sam Walton, and Steve Jobs in the world, who will create radically better educational programs than the government monopoly. There will be a full range of product offerings from Family Dollar to Neiman Marcus versus one monolithic system that is supposed to serve all students and effectively serves none.

The good news is private for-profit schools may emerge despite the hundreds of billions of dollars in subsidies being poured into the public school system. The best analogy is the U.S. Post Office. There are entrepreneurs ready to build a UPS and a FedEx to compete with the government schools. Private schools based on technology and curriculum properly combined will seriously challenge the government schools in the next 10 to 15 years.

Capital

The second pillar of human productivity is the tools, machines, equipment, and computer programs, collectively called "capital," that magnify the production process. If our task is to move 100 tons of dirt 500 yards and I have a well-functioning bulldozer and you have a shovel, I will win. In fact, I will work dramatically less than you do and accomplish much more. Tools (capital) radically enhance human productivity.

Tools are the product of the human mind. Someone has to invent the bulldozer or the iPad. Tools are created by innovative, focused, committed human minds. Government regulations are often the enemy of this creative process. Societies with freer markets and less government regulation do a far better job creating the tools and technology that advance human flourishing.

The human mind plays another important role in the creation of tools (capital). Someone has to choose to save for there to be capital (which is necessary for tool creation). With what you produce, you can either consume or save (which by definition becomes an investment that is capital). If you eat all your corn, you will not have any seed corn to plant next year's crop. Some human mind must be willing to forgo current consumption to provide the capital that enables the investment in the creation of a bulldozer, which may take years to produce. High taxes on savings (including dividends and capital gains) reduce capital creation, which reduces the rate of investment in new tools and thereby slows progress and reduces human flourishing. As in all economic activity, when progress slows in the advanced economies, the greatest negative impact is in the poorest economies that are fundamentally dependent on capital creation in wealthier societies. Raise taxes on capital gains in one of the developed countries and slow economic growth in Bangladesh.

It is amazing how confused (or intentionally misleading) liberal/progressive economists are in regard to capital creation. From Karl Marx forward, they have somehow disconnected capital creation from labor. In fact, all capital is created by mental labor, the human mind, as just described. Effectively, they are glorifying physical labor at the expense of mental labor, when in reality the mind of a human is his means of survival, success, and happiness. Anyone interested in using bare hands to move that 100 tons of dirt described earlier? After all, even a shovel is a tool that was invented by human mental labor.

The progressive/liberal economists try to separate the return on capital from the return on labor, failing to realize that all capital is created by mental labor. Microsoft, Walmart, Apple, Google, and Amazon.com were all started with small capital investments. The businesses grew by retaining earnings—reinvesting profits. It was the choice of the human minds of the owners to save (to reinvest their earnings) that allowed these businesses to grow.

Instead of the destructive, misleading conception of a conflict between capital and labor as argued by the progressive/liberal economists, capital is created by human mental labor and radically increases the productivity of all labor, including physical labor, thereby improving human well-being. Attacks on capital conducted by progressive/liberal intellectuals and politicians are attacks on human flourishing. The people that are hurt the most are the poorest throughout the world.

If you work for a business, the tools (capital) will typically be provided by the firm from the investment of the owners (shareholders). The better tools you have to work with, the more productive you can be. In today's world, the most impactful tools are often information/technology, which are possible because of capital investments. In most businesses, the vast majority of capital comes from retained profits. Typically, a substantial portion of profits are reinvested (retained) in the business. Profits enable the creation of the tools that magnify human productivity. Profits are essential to human well-being. If your company is not profitable, it will not be able to invest in the tools (information/technology) that make you productive.

At the societal level there is an analogy with the retained profits that allow a business to invest in tools that increase productivity. In the total economy, net savings are equivalent to retained profits at the firm level. Individuals can either save (invest) or consume their income. The same is true for firms and governments. Individuals, firms, and governments can also finance consumption and investment by borrowing. That borrowing must be repaid from future production/income. An individual can borrow for additional education. The question is whether this additional education will improve her future productivity (income) to cover the cost of education and the loss of income while she is in school. Of course, anyone may take an art course for the pure enjoyment. This is a form of consumption that is certainly acceptable, if you can afford this expense.

If a firm borrows, the question is whether the resources/tools it purchases will increase its productivity/income enough to more than repay the cost of borrowing.

Unfortunately, at the federal government level, the vast majority of borrowings are for current consumption, not for investment. This means that a portion of the savings (capital) that individuals and firms are creating is being consumed, instead of invested, by the federal government. The United States is borrowing from foreigners to finance current consumption. The challenge will be to repay these borrowings when investment in future productivity is less than it would have been. This issue is magnified by the commitment the federal government and many states have made to pay for future consumption (Social Security, Medicare, Medicaid, state pension plans) while at the same time reducing current capital accumulation.

Incentives

The third pillar of human productivity is incentives. Incentives can be economic and/or psychological/spiritual. Incentives matter. One of the few resolved issues in economics is that incentives impact behavior. Anyone who has run a business knows that incentives have a radical impact on outcomes. Bad incentives produce destructive outcomes. Effective incentives produce desirable outcomes.

Leadership is primarily about incentives. This book does not utilize that terminology; nevertheless, vision, purpose, strategy, and values are all forms of incentives when seen in the broadest context. Much of the context of the book is about individual and organizational incentives.

The role of incentives is probably self-evident to you in terms of your personal productivity. Those incentives may be psychological or material (typically money). Many people spend much time and energy on projects that are personally rewarding in intangible ways. In a business environment, psychological reward/recognition is often a very powerful incentive.

Of course, economic incentives are significant drivers of efforts that produce results. At the firm level, it is critically important that incentives, both psychological and economic, be aligned to accomplish the mission of the organization. Misaligned incentives can be extraordinarily destructive.

At this point the primary focus will be to review societal incentives and disincentives in relation to the question raised at the start of this chapter as to why the U.S. economy is not growing faster.

Does raising marginal income tax rates on high-income individuals increase or decrease incentives for production? Does threatening to raise tax rates further increase or decrease the incentives for production? Does raising taxes on dividends and capital gains increase or decrease the desire and ability to invest? (After all, most capital is created by after-tax retained earnings. Higher taxes and less-retained earnings equal less capital.) Does radically increasing regulatory cost and regulatory risk increase or decrease the incentive to innovate and take risk? Does passing massive new laws (for example, the Patient Protection and Affordable Care Act, commonly known as Obamacare, and the Dodd-Frank Wall Street Reform and Consumer Protection Act, commonly known as Dodd-Frank) with many unknown regulatory implications, thereby creating ambiguity, increase or decrease the willingness of businesses to expand and create jobs? Does arbitrarily changing the law by executive fiat (Obamacare), thereby producing more uncertainty, increase or decrease the desire of small business owners to take the plunge and grow their business?

Does calling business leaders "villains" and "greedy capitalists" increase or decrease their desire to expand and take risk? Does telling entrepreneurs that "you didn't do it; we did it," increase or decrease their motivation to invest?

Of course, in every case, these incentives decrease the willingness and ability of business leaders to innovate, invest, and create jobs. It is hard to believe the U.S. economy is growing at all given these disincentives. However, as the original comments noted, the United States should be booming with the combination of technological advancements, the benefits of freer global trade, and especially the U.S. energy revolution. It is a shame that the cost of these disincentives creates such a tremendous lost opportunity.

The ultimate societal incentive is freedom. Once basic (and limited) rule of law is established, liberty is the most empowering incentive of all. (See the Cato Institute website: http://www.Human Progress.org.) We will discuss the role of liberty in human flourishing in future chapters.

In the long term, we cannot consume more than we produce. The real economic issue is production—that is, productivity. The three pillars for productivity at the individual, firm, and societal level are knowledge, tools (capital), and incentives.

If you are serious about accomplishing your personal purpose, do you have the knowledge to achieve this objective? If not, what can you do to systematically obtain this knowledge? Do you have the tools (capital) to achieve your purpose? If not, what can you do to obtain those tools? Can you borrow capital to this end? Do you have both the psychological and financial incentives to attain your ambition?

In your business, do the employees, especially the leaders, have the knowledge and the right combination of knowledge (know-how) to provide better products and services to your clients? Has the firm invested adequately in employee knowledge creation to ensure competitive advantage? Can the leadership of the firm effectively integrate the accumulated knowledge of the individuals in the firm? Has the firm provided the tools (and raised the capital to finance the tools) that will maximize the productivity of the individual employees and created the environment whereby employees can optimize the integration of their individual activities? Are the psychological and economic incentives truly designed to encourage behavior that optimizes the achievement of the company's mission? Do the employees have the freedom (creativity) to do their job productively? Psychological incentives are often underestimated.

Since productivity drives economic well-being and there is much evidence that being productive is an important component in the pursuit of happiness, legitimate questions for you to ask in evaluating public policies are: Do these policies optimize the productivity of the individuals in the society? Are the candidates you vote for supporting the type of policies that create productivity, or are they primarily focused on redistribution? You make a choice.

7

Honesty

HONESTY IS A FOUNDATIONAL VIRTUE. WITHOUT HONESTY IT IS impossible to create successful relationships. Without honesty there cannot be trust. Most of the ethical issues visible in society are some form of dishonesty. To be dishonest is to be disconnected from reality, which is a very unhealthy place to be.

It is appropriate to reflect on the standard of honesty. Many people think that being honest is about being correct. However, as human beings, we are not omniscient. We can be honest and be wrong, because we do not know everything.

There is a rigorous standard for honesty. That standard is: we must say what we mean and know what we mean. Saying what you mean requires that you do not intentionally mislead people. I doubt that anyone reading this book does that very often at the meta level. If you do, you will soon have significant problems.

On the other hand, at the micro level many individuals are not fully honest. The cumulative effect of "white" lies is a "black" lie. This behavior is observable in some managers. Tom will tell his manager that Suzy has a performance problem. However, when Tom does Suzy's annual performance review, he sugarcoats the negatives because he does not enjoy providing negative feedback. Later, Tom becomes angry at Suzy because she did not hear what he did not say.

Have you ever become angry at a friend because she did not hear what you did not say? Have you ever become angry with your spouse because he or she did not hear what you did not say?

It is irrational to expect someone to change his or her behavior based on nonexistent feedback. Also, why are you unwilling to express this negative belief? Do you want to hold a grudge? Are you unclear that your negative judgment is accurate, and yet you continue to hold the opinion and act accordingly? Obviously, there are times when you are in the process of developing an opinion, but if you are willing to express a negative opinion about a subordinate or friend to a manager or another friend, you should be willing to express that opinion directly to the individual. This will allow the individual to refute your position, change his or her behavior, or provide an explanation that may change the context in which you make your judgment.

The second and equally important aspect of honesty is that you must "know what you mean." As human beings we are not omniscient, and "know what you mean" does not require omniscience, but it does require that you do not claim knowledge you do not have. Have you ever been in a group meeting where an individual claimed to be certain about some factor that caused the group to make a specific decision, and then later it turned out that the individual had misled the group? Have you ever been that person?

Once you have claimed knowledge, it is difficult to undo the claim. You may start rationalizing your incorrect position. Sometimes the best answer is "I do not know." This answer does not mislead others and may motivate you to learn the answer. Once you claim knowledge you do not have, there is a natural propensity to defend the position you have taken even in the face of contradictory evidence.

Of course, there are many situations where you are expressing probabilities such as "I think," "maybe," "possibly," or "the most likely outcome is x." All are reasonable expressions under the appropriate circumstance, but the level of certainty needs to be clear.

More damage may be done by claims to knowledge one does not have than pure deception. Deception (dishonesty) can be very destructive in the short term, but typically, although not always, reality exposes deceptions. Untrue knowledge claims are more easily disguised after the fact and the perpetrator afforded the opportunity to make similar claims in the future. Politicians, public policy analysts, and academic scholars often make claims of knowledge that are not justified and lead to destructive decisions.

There is rapidly increasing evidence of exaggerated claims to knowledge from the scientific (or pseudoscientific) community. Observe the numerous misleading healthcare claims. Early in my bank lending career, many small-farm egg producers were put out of business by the claim that eating eggs was terribly bad for you. It turns out that eating some eggs is good for you. How about AIA in apple juices, which was said to "poison" schoolchildren? It turns out apple juice is good for you. Coffee was bad, now is good. And so forth. According to Jeff Tollefson in the January 2014 issue of *Nature*, the earth's temperature has not risen in 17 years. This is a serious problem for the claimed certainty of the climate change movement, as 100 percent of its models have been incorrect. Many scientific claims are being made based on statistical correlations instead of causality. While statistical correlations can be valuable, they do not prove causation. This is especially true when the sample size is small and the test period relatively short. One factor that may be driving this outcome is government funding of scientific research. People seem to understand that if an industry funds research, the objectivity of the researcher may be in question. However, somehow if research is government funded, it must be objective. Not so. Government bureaucrats have biases that can easily be communicated to researchers who understand what the expected outcome should be.

Dishonesty cannot be tolerated in organizations. Dishonesty destroys both trust and relationships. In fact, honesty is the foundation for trust, which is essential for any form of successful relationships. I have often told recent college graduates that the most important personal attribute they need to initially demonstrate in their new job is trustworthiness. If you make a mistake, it is critically important that you own the mistake and let your manager know that you made the mistake. She will find out anyway. If she finds out from someone else that you made a mistake and you chose to not disclose the mistake, she will not trust you. By the way, since you are on a learning curve, she expects you to make mistakes anyway. She just wonders if you have the intestinal fortitude to admit your mistakes. It is generally permissible to let your manager know about your accomplishments (without embellishment), but it is more important to let her know about your failures. Also knowing you will disclose your failures to your manager is a healthy form of discipline as long as this does not keep you from taking rational risk. By the way, you are going to make mistakes if you do anything worth doing.

If you cannot trust someone, it is impossible to effectively work with that person toward meaningful goals. Honesty creates trust. Lack of honesty destroys trust. As in most issues, there is always room for judgment in assessing honesty. People can simply be mistaken. They can miscommunicate or be confused. However, overt dishonesty or a pattern of dishonesty cannot be tolerated at work or in raising your children. Intentional half-truths are very destructive, especially when they are self-serving. Individuals who are dishonest should not be allowed to continue to be part of the team, even if they appear to be productive. Their dishonesty ultimately will be destructive to the team.

It is noteworthy that we seem to tolerate a level of dishonesty in politicians that we would not tolerate at work or with our friends. Why is this? Do we choose to support candidates because they are saying what we wish was true even though at some level we know it is not true?

A recent example stands out, although there are many examples from both political parties. President Barack Obama claimed on numerous occasions in regard to the Affordable Care Act that "you can keep your insurance" when he must have known, or absolutely should have known, that millions of individuals would in fact lose their current insurance coverage. The law was designed to eliminate certain types of insurance policies the president did not view as appropriate. This was a serious false claim (a form of dishonesty) that almost certainly impacted election results. The president lost some public support when this dishonesty was disclosed, but not nearly as much as he should have lost, given the level of impact. A CEO with a similar level of intensity and repetitiveness of a false claim would almost certainly be dismissed and possibly subject to legal action. It is appropriate to emphasize that President Obama is not unique in this type of behavior by politicians.

Honesty is essential in individual human relationships because it makes trust possible. If you cannot trust your spouse or she or he cannot trust you, the relationship will surely die unless trust can be restored. In business, if employees cannot be trusted, they will need to be dismissed, or the organization will be seriously damaged. If you cannot trust your manager, figure out how to get a new manager or change jobs or companies.

One of my themes is that the same sets of principles that are applicable for individual happiness are also essential for organizational success and for societal flourishing. If we tolerate dishonesty in our political leaders, we are laying the foundation for an unsuccessful society. Isn't it more significant that political leaders of either party be fundamentally honest than whether they appear to be sociable, nice, and "caring"? Would you want to create a friendship with someone who appears to be caring but is actually dishonest and untrustworthy? Since political leaders in our mixed economy have such a significant impact on the lives of millions of people, and as honesty is a fundamental value, should not the standard for honesty be higher than that imposed on private individuals and business leaders instead of lower?

I had a personal lesson about honesty early in my business career. I was responsible for preparing a past-due loan report that was presented by a higher-level manager to the executive committee of the board of the bank. On this occasion, after the report was prepared the manager called me into his office. The past dues had increased significantly, and he knew the executive committee would not be pleased. He asked me to change the report because he said a large past-due loan had been made current after the date of the report. I refused to change the report since it was on a specific date. Of course, he could tell the executive committee what he had told me, but the report needed to be factually correct. He was infuriated, and I thought my career at the bank might be over. It turned out that the past-due borrower had made only a partial payment and subsequently went into default, and we had to foreclose. Whether anyone would have figured out the report was false was unclear, but I would have known. I am certain that if I had fudged this report, I would still feel bad about the decision to this day. The "guilt" may have impacted the rest of my career. It is unclear what is cause and effect, but this manager subsequently left the organization and was terminated in several future jobs and had severe psychological problems.

In complete candor, at the time I was making only $625 per month, unmarried, and living in a small eastern North Carolina tobacco market town. So I did not have a lot to lose if the manager had forced me out of the organization. The more you have to lose, the harder this type of decision may become, but if you have decided to be uncompromisingly honest, you do not have to consider the superficial trade-offs. Also, once you have made a set of decisions where your honesty puts you at risk and yet you know being honest is the right decision and self-rewarding, then you automate honest behavior.

One of the most important aspects of honesty is keeping agreements. Violating an agreement is a form of dishonesty. This makes it very important not to enter into agreements you cannot keep. It also requires that you clearly specify the terms of the agreement where practical and be sure the other party is also aligned with the terms of the agreement.

Legal agreements can play a significant role, but in my experience this type of contract often is the least effective. A clear verbal agreement documented with a relatively short letter (if necessary) is typically a more effective contract. The spirit of an agreement is a defining context for the written document.

During my tenure as CEO at BB&T, the bank became the preferred acquisitor of community banks. There are a number of reasons why this occurred, which I will outline later, but a primary factor was that we always kept our agreements. When we were discussing the possibility of a financial institution selling to BB&T, we would refer the CEO of the merger prospect to the CEOs of the many companies we had previously acquired. We knew those CEOs would always tell the prospect that we had kept our agreements, because we always kept our agreements.

Since it was our responsibility to be sure the agreement was clear, if after the merger had occurred, the CEO of the company we had acquired raised a legitimate issue that was unclear, but where it would increase the cost to BB&T, we would also pay up. At that point, the merged CEO practically had no power since this was an undocumented aspect of the agreement. However, the spirit of the agreement was the real contract. I think our actions to be fair when we technically did not have to act were far more important to our reputation than the legal contract. Of course, a few times individuals made unreasonable requests that were not within the context of the original agreements, and we did not comply. But these occurrences were rare.

Failure to keep agreements is a form of dishonesty, and it should be treated accordingly.

8

Integrity

THERE ARE MANY APPARENT TEMPTATIONS IN LIFE. HOWEVER, IF you have developed your principles logically and consistently, those apparent temptations are not really temptations. They are just ways to fail. Integrity is fundamentally the harmony of mind and body. As a principle, it guides us to act consistently with our beliefs.

Unfortunately, many people do not act with integrity. This is typically because they hold beliefs inconsistent with reality and/or inconsistent with their other beliefs. You cannot act consistently with concepts that are inconsistent with reality. If you act in a way inconsistent with reality for long, you will die. These types of beliefs simply make you feel guilty. You cannot act consistently with contradictory beliefs. Attempting to act consistently with contradictory concepts will make you unhappy and guilty because you will be wrong in some sense, no matter how you choose to act.

Whether or not you agree with any other thoughts in this book, if you want to act with integrity, you must have a set of values that are consistent with reality and are not contradictory. Please reflect on your value system accordingly.

Many people view integrity as some form of duty. Integrity is not a duty. It is a means to improve the probability of being successful and happy. The concept is to develop your principles outside the "heat of battle" and then to consistently apply those principles in the heat of battle because you know that living these principles improves the probability of being successful and happy. Therefore, it is important to not view integrity as a duty or some kind of ill-defined obligation. This perception encourages you to "cheat" on the very principles that are fundamental to your success and happiness. Of course, at the risk of being redundant, your principles must be designed to promote your life or you will violate them and feel guilty and be less successful. Developing and accepting the correct principles is critical.

Integrity is a long-term concept. This is particularly important to understand in the current environment of immediate satisfaction. There are decisions that may be in your short-term benefit that will be very destructive in the long term. I tell college students that they should make decisions consistent with a life expectancy of 100 years. Integrity requires that one hold the long-term context. At my age, you realize the long term will arrive radically faster than you think it will.

Integrity, like all values, is contextual. In a certain context one should absolutely never compromise one's principles, because these principles are the foundation for success and happiness. There are many compromises in the content of life. We often compromise with our spouses on the selection of movies or the choice of restaurants. In business-to-business transactions, price negotiations (compromises) are standard practice. However, never compromise the context, never compromise your principles, which are designed to promote your well-being.

Even though values in the context of normal life are not negotiable, in extraordinary circumstances they are flexible. Remember, the purpose of values is to promote your life. They are not duties. If someone puts a gun to your head and says, "If you do not tell me I am beautiful, I will shoot you," then even though you honestly do not view this individual as beautiful, you should say, "I think you are beautiful." When force is applied, the normal principles are not applicable. The concept is that fundamental values are absolute in normal life circumstances, but they are not necessarily applicable when force of some kind is involved.

Although, as with all values, integrity is an attribute of individuals, organizations/societies encourage or discourage individuals to act with integrity. Unfortunately, businesses often do not have values consistent with reality and consistent with one another. They may make politically correct promises that are not achievable in a globally competitive environment, which makes these values inconsistent with reality. Often in a corporation's mission statement the business will outline commitments that are practically incompatible with one another. They may make save-the-planet commitments that consist of using recycled paper while the CEO travels the globe in a corporate jet. There is nothing wrong with the CEO traveling the world in a corporate jet, unless it is inconsistent with the value proposition the organization is promoting.

The test of a rational mission and values statement for a business is whether it is achievable in the real world and whether the concepts expressed are consistent with one another. A truly effective mission statement will consider all the firm's primary constituents, but it will recognize that achieving a satisfactory profit is mandatory in a competitive global economy. Detached from reality, altruistic claims are especially destructive. Employees will try to figure out what the organization's real mission and values are based on actual experience. If the real mission/values are different from the stated mission/values, employees will face a cognitive disconnect, which will make it harder for them to be psychologically incented to be productive.

In the same context, societies have implicit mission and values statements that are open to interpretation. The United States is the first country founded on an explicit philosophy expressed in the Declaration of Independence and codified in the U.S. Constitution. The American Revolution was far more significant philosophically than militarily. The American Founding Fathers held that rights belong to individuals, not the government. In fact, governments exist for the purpose of protecting individual rights: life, liberty, and the pursuit of happiness. When the Founding Fathers proclaimed that all men were "created equal," they meant all men had equal rights before the law. They were not advocates of equal opportunity or equal outcome. You have the right to what you produce, but you cannot have the right to what others produce. While government had a proactive role in a few areas, such as the military, its primary role was the protection of individual rights. Government, therefore, had only limited and enumerated powers. It was not responsible for eliminating all the problems in society. These community problems were to be solved by private individuals and voluntary, charitable institutions. You can consider the Declaration of Independence and the Constitution as the original vision, mission, and values statement for the United States.

In the late 1800s a new view of the mission statement of the U.S. government and the related value statement began to evolve. This was the Progressive Movement, which was an offshoot of Bismarck's Germany and its social welfare compact. That, by the way, ultimately metamorphosed into National Socialism (Nazism). In the Progressive vision and mission, government has a dramatically enlarged role. It is basically responsible for solving all of society's problems. The measure of performance is no longer an individual's rights but the welfare of the community (the community as defined by the Progressives). The goal was no longer equality before the law but egalitarianism in the context of equal outcomes. From each according to his ability, to each according to his needs, is how Marx would describe this principle, although the Progressives dance around this definition.

The Founding Fathers' concept of government's role as very limited and potentially dangerous versus the Progressive's vision of government as the ultimate source of well-being are not consistent. The current level of political strife in the United States is partly driven by the conflict between these two visions and the related values implications.

We do have multiple test cases of these competing visions: Eastern Europe versus Western Europe, North Korea versus South Korea, and the Soviet Union versus the United States. There are numerous studies that show an extremely high correlation between societies that respect individual rights, especially property rights, and economic well-being. We can, therefore, be certain that economic and political freedom produce better outcomes for everyone, but the outcomes are unequal.

To have integrity, an individual, an organization, and a society must have a set of principles that is consistent with life on this earth and consistent with one another. At the societal level this type of consistency is a gigantic challenge and will probably never be fully achieved. However, to the degree societal leaders and political parties hold views on human life that are logically inconsistent, they will be significantly less effective, and well-being will suffer accordingly. Leaders who believe in economic freedom but not civil liberty, or civil liberty but not economic freedom, are enemies of societal integrity. Think about it.

Justice

In human relationships, justice is typically the number one value. Reflect on your reaction when you feel unjustly criticized. Justice, properly defined, is the virtue of judging a person's character and conduct objectively and of acting accordingly, granting to each individual that which she deserves.

In organizations, ask someone what he thinks about his manager and soon he will describe his manager as fair or unfair, just or unjust. Individuals do not want to work for someone who underrewards performance or overrewards unproductive results. They are right to feel that way. In addition, if there is not a reward for superior performance, the best people will leave and the organization will be worse off. Furthermore, if there is not a reward for superior performance, the average person will not be motivated to perform at an above-average level. One very important role of leaders is to encourage average people to perform at an above-average level.

Individuals should be evaluated and rewarded objectively (for better or worse) based on their contributions toward accomplishing the organization's mission and adherence to its values. Those who contribute the most should receive the most.

At BB&T, we had incentive compensation systems all the way down to the teller line. Measuring performance is part science and part art. However, the goal is clear: those who contribute the most should receive the most.

Based on this concept of justice, egalitarianism should be consciously rejected. Equal opportunity as used by egalitarians is an oxymoron. Michael Jordan was born with better legs for jumping than me—do we have equal opportunity? In addition, egalitarians are not genuinely arguing for equal opportunity, whatever that means, but are arguing for equal outcomes.

Certainly, everyone should be equal before the law. In addition, absent any negative information, all human beings deserve to be treated with respect simply because they are human beings. However, everyone is not equal. In fact, I have never met two equal people. Every individual is a unique, special person. We each have different abilities, motivations, insights, strengths, and weaknesses. This is the good news. We are all individuals. We are all special people. At the extreme, Thomas Edison and the Boston Strangler are not equal.

Because individuals are not equal, it is necessary to judge people. We must make judgments in many areas. Are we eating the best food for us, wearing appropriate clothes, purchasing the correct car? Do we work for the right manager, do we have the right employees, are we marrying the best person for us, do our children have the right friends? In fact, judging (evaluating) other people is one of the most important sets of decisions you must make to promote your life and happiness. Therefore, how you evaluate other people is critically important.

The appropriate method to evaluate other people is: (1) as individuals, (2) based on their personal merits, and (3) in the context of the specific situation for which the judgment is being made. Someone might make a good friend for you but not be qualified for a specific job in your company.

Because there is a proper method for judging individuals and because individuals must be evaluated as individuals (because they are individuals), collectivism and all its ugly variations should be rejected. Collectivists judge individuals by their membership in groups. Since all the individuals in the group are different and therefore should be judged differently, collectivists have a 100 percent error rate.

Forms of collectivism include racism, sexism, communism, social-ism, and nationalism. You will note these forms of collectivism span the political spectrum. Many individuals on the right are national-ists, whereas many on the left are socialists. This fact highlights that the real distinction is between collectivists who view people as cogs in a collective wheel and individualists who recognize that in reality there are only concrete individuals. Groups are abstractions. There is no such thing as the proletariat. Using the concept of group mem-bership can be an interesting tool as long as one realizes in reality there are only individuals.

In business, the most common forms of collectivism are racism and sexism. In my career there has been some progress, but there are still many racists and sexists. There are probably a number of factors that motivate people to become racist or sexist, but one clear factor is low self-esteem. The mindset is: "I may have many weaknesses, but my group (race/sex/nationality) is better than yours."

What racists and sexists fail to realize is that racism and sex-ism are both unjust to the person being discriminated against and destructive to the person doing the discrimination. For example, if BB&T has a branch manager who refuses to hire the best per-son for the job because that person is male, female, black, white, Chinese, or any other nonessential reason, that branch will be less successful than it would have been. If she continues this pattern, the branch will be so unsuccessful she will be fired, which is a form of justice.

Irrational discrimination is not only unjust to the person being discriminated against but also self-destructive to the person doing the irrational discrimination. This points to a very important gen-eral principle: our means of survival, success, and happiness is our capacity to think rationally. One of the most important areas in which we must think rationally is our judgment of other people. If we judge people for irrational reasons, there will be negative conse-quences for us.

There has been much discussion about the negative consequences of racism and sexism. However, the issue is both more subtle and broader. If you judge someone for any nonessential reason, there will be negative consequences. For the vast majority of purposes, the length of someone's hair, his style of dress, whether he is a vegetarian or not, and multiple other factors are not relevant. When speaking to college students, I tell them that if they choose their future spouse by how good he or she looks instead of by his or her character, bad things will happen in the long term.

One of the more destructive trends currently in the United States is a rising focus on social class. Class warfare truly is a collectivist mindset. Evaluating individuals by their membership in a class, whatever that is, is as irrational as judging them by their race or sex.

Justice is a two-edged sword. Justice requires that we reward superior performance. Most business leaders either understand this concept or they lose their best performers and ultimately go out of business. Unfortunately, there is a different reaction at the societal level where superior results are sometimes vilified. Not rewarding superior performance at the societal level will reduce the standard of living for everyone.

Justice also requires that we deal with nonperformance. Failing to deal with nonperformance is an injustice. Nonperformers hurt the other members of the team or organization. It is not fair to the performing members of the team to have to carry the nonperformers. Equally important, it is not fair to the nonperformer. I have never met a happy nonperformer. Failing to deal with nonperformance is unfair to the nonperformer. People are not going to be happy in a task they are not qualified to perform. And in a free market, practically everybody can have an opportunity to be productive if they are focused on work they are capable of doing.

When speaking to university students when professors are also in the audience, I point out that if a professor gives a student a better grade than she deserves, the professor has done the student a disservice. The student believes she knows more than she knows, which is not healthy. Also, knowledge is cumulative, so not achieving mastery at a lower level impacts the ability to achieve mastery at a higher level. Grade inflation in universities is a form of injustice. The truly outstanding performers are not able to differentiate their performance from the others, and the low performers think they are capable of tasks they are not prepared to do.

Another thought about justice: it only applies to human action. Mother Nature is neither just nor unjust. She just is. Railing against Mother Nature is a waste of time and energy.

Let's examine justice at the individual, organizational, and societal levels. At the individual level, the most rewarding relationships you can create are with individuals who share your values and at least some of your interests. Justice would require you reward these relationships with time, attention, and positive support in proportion to the rewards you receive from the relationship. Relationships without shared values or shared interests may survive, but generally they are not healthy to either party.

In an organizational setting, individuals should be judged based on their adherence to the agreed-upon values of the organization (their character) and their performance toward accomplishing the mission of the organization. Adherence to values and character is more important than performance. People can sometimes produce superior tangible results in the short term, but if they have a character flaw, they will do considerable damage in the long term. Being merciless on values issues is justice in an organizational context. (And, of course, there are gray areas.)

How do we convert the concepts of justice at the personal level and at the organizational level into justice at the societal level? Let's face the fact that everyone is for justice. We just have many different concepts of what justice looks like, and it seems difficult for many people to convert the principles that they apply to their individual relationships and use in the organizations in which they participate to society as a whole. There is a disconnect between the principles of individual justice and justice in the collective that is not conceptually valid.

Let's discuss justice in regard to money. Those of us who believe in liberty also believe that all of us are entitled to whatever we receive as long as the exchange is voluntary and as long as force is not used to create the exchange. (Fraud is a form of force.) For example, some movie actors and some athletes make substantial amounts of money. But you are not forced to attend a movie or go to a baseball game. The fact that outstanding athletes or movie actresses make a tremendous amount of money is not an injustice. They have earned the money through voluntary exchange of values. In going to the baseball game, we typically do not make a judgment of the baseball player's political philosophy. We are focused on his performance as an athlete within the agreed-upon rules of the game.

Highly compensated CEOs also are paid based on voluntary exchange. Boards may make poor decisions in terms of individual compensation, but the exchange is voluntary. So the determination of justice in economics is whether the individual receives her compensation based on voluntary exchange, not the amount of compensation. For those of us who believe in freedom, the question of justice is all about voluntary exchange. If force or fraud is involved, then an injustice has occurred. There is overwhelming evidence that when voluntary exchange is the principle, most people directly involved have a sense that justice has been done. This perception of justice is one of the reasons that societies that are primarily driven by voluntary exchange are more successful for all individuals.

Unfortunately, in a mixed economy as exists in the United States today, this sense of justice can become blurred, which can lead to destructive public policies. A mixed economy is best described as crony statism. The typically expressed term is crony capitalism, but this is an oxymoron. In a true capitalist economy, the government does not and cannot dole out favors to businesses or pressure groups. The economic system we have today is not capitalism.

The problem in a crony statist economy is that force is often being used to impact economic outcomes. Why did Wall Street CEOs whose firms had failed get bailed out using taxpayer money? Why did pension plans of union employees at auto firms get bailed out at the expense of other General Motors creditors (including other nonunion pension plans)? Why are a handful of very wealthy sugar producers able to receive massive subsidies at the expense of higher prices to all consumers, including poor people? Why do solar energy contractors receive massive government subsidies while coal miners lose their jobs based on government energy policies? Why can a welfare recipient who maximizes her benefits in Hawaii receive $62,000 annually (according to a 2013 Cato White Paper, "The Work Versus Welfare Trade-Off," by Michael D. Tanner and Charles Hughes) while an individual who works full-time in the same state makes only $36,920? Why was Boeing able to renegotiate the contract for new refueling jets at a substantial increase in cost to taxpayers? And on and on.

What makes government action fundamentally different than private action is that our government has a gun. It can put you in jail or kill you if you do not obey. By the way, far more individuals have been killed by government than by criminals throughout history. In fact, except from diseases of all types, the largest cause of death throughout history has been some kind of action by government, including wars. Government, by definition, violates the voluntary exchange principle. You probably did not volunteer to subsidize wealthy sugar producers, did you?

When the voluntary exchange principle is violated, the concept of justice goes out the window and the concept of power (force) walks in the door. Society then becomes a series of competing groups, which can ultimately destroy economic well-being.

It is critical to understand that the common good (or the public interest) is an indefinable concept. There is no such thing as the public. The public is only a number of individual people. As Ayn Rand stated in "The Common Good," when the common good of a society is regarded as something apart from and superior to the individual good of its members, the good of some people takes precedence over the good of other people, with those others reduced to the status of sacrificial animals.

The greater the common good that is proclaimed by statists, the more difficult it is for most people to bring this misleading abstract concept back to reality. (Remember, even the most complex ideas should be traceable back to reality.)

Let's take the issue of wealth redistribution. You live in a neighborhood where there are 10 families and where there is uneven income. One family has an annual income of $40,000, and another family, $200,000. Several progressive/liberal neighbors organize a neighborhood gathering, and 6 families vote to force the $200,000 income family to give $20,000 a year to the lowest-income family, $10,000 to the next lowest, and $5,000 to the next two families. The high-income family refuses to pay, and the neighborhood committee members get their guns to ensure justice is done. Do you think the high-income family will move? Will they get guns? Will they bribe some of their neighbors to change their vote? Do you want to live in this neighborhood? By the way, the high-income family may have been willing to help the lowest income-family voluntarily, but no one asked them to.

The scale (300 million+ people) and the process (Congress) do not change the implications of the use of force even if the majority can be convinced the use of force is for the common good. This is especially true when some of the majority benefit from the use of force.

Let me tell you a story to integrate some concepts and to illustrate why egalitarianism is such a destructive idea. The selection of this story tells you something about where I went to college and my age. One of my heroes is Michael Jordan. He is one of the greatest basketball players of all time, maybe the best. He also was an inspiration to poor children.

This will surprise you, but I am not as good a basketball player as Michael Jordan. In fact, no matter how hard I tried and you tried to help me, I cannot become as good a basketball player as Michael Jordan. You cannot make the average great. You can help the average become better, which is often a worthwhile endeavor. But the average cannot become great. However, you can make the great average. In reality, the only way to make people equal is to make the great average, because you cannot make the average great. For this reason, egalitarians must be in the business of making the great average.

It is simple to make Michael Jordan as good a basketball player as me—cut his legs off. You say we would not cut his legs off. I don't know. People have been tough on the great people throughout history: they poisoned Socrates, imprisoned Galileo, and burned Joan of Arc. Today, we are more sophisticated, at least in Western civilization (not so in some parts of the world). We use balls and chains, in the form of high tax rates and mind-numbing rules and regulations. According to the Congressional Budget Office and the IRS, the top 1 percent of taxpayers pay 35 percent of all federal income taxes. The top 5 percent pay 57 percent. More than 40 percent of individuals with earned income pay no federal income taxes—an interesting culture for a democracy.

What many people fail to realize is that great individuals make a disproportionate contribution to human well-being. Everyone reading this book, your children and grandchildren, all have a better life thanks to Thomas Edison. Edison invented the lightbulb, phonograph, electrical generator, the research laboratory, and much more. Put balls and chains on great people and reduce the quality of life for all of us.

Egalitarians like to claim the moral high ground. After all, who can argue about us all being equal? However, what really motivates egalitarians is the most destructive of all human emotions—envy. Envy is a form of hatred of the good for being the good. Watch envy in yourself. Egalitarianism is an attack on the best based on the destructive psychology of envy, rationalized as justice.

Egalitarianism, like altruism, carried to its logical conclusion reduces performance to the lowest level. Remember, one-half of the population is below average in any specific field. I am clearly below average in music. My music performance cannot be raised to average. Therefore, the only way for me to be equal is to reduce the music ability of even the average individuals.

Egalitarianism is a very destructive ideal.

Pride

ARISTOTLE TAUGHT THAT PRIDE WAS THE GREATEST OF ALL VIRTUES because to earn it you had to have all the other virtues—rationality, independent thinking, productivity, honesty, integrity, justice, and so on. As such, pride serves an important role. It is a psychological reminder to behave consistently with your other values and a psychological reward for doing so.

When talking to student groups about pride, I request that the students ask themselves two questions when they are faced with the next ethical decision (and ethical decisions occur fairly often): Would you tell the people you value, not the newspapers, but the people you have judged to be important in your life, what you are going to do? And would you explain why you are going to do it? If you would not tell the people you have determined to be valuable to you what you are going to do and why you are going to do it, don't do it. This is because you will always know what you did, and far more important, you will know why you did it. You always want to be able to be proud of yourself. Obviously, doing something that you are not proud of, even if you do not get caught, makes it impossible to be proud of yourself.

Pride is often described as a deadly sin instead of the greatest virtue. When pride is viewed in a negative light, it is typically false pride or arrogance that is being criticized. It is certainly true that individuals take credit for results they have not achieved. This is a form of dishonesty and is rightly criticized.

Arrogance is an overestimation of one's character and/or abilities. Arrogance is very dangerous, because it can result in fake or misplaced confidence, which often results in irrational decisions. Also, arrogant individuals typically have difficulty accepting negative feedback and often blame others for their failures. Taking credit for what someone else has achieved or blaming others for your mistakes is false pride or arrogance. In Aristotle's context you must earn your right to be proud of yourself through ethical behavior by being a person of character.

One of the virtues we have discussed is productivity. In an organizational context, to be objectively proud of yourself you must be productive toward the accomplishment of the mission of the organization. So in order to be proud of yourself in an organizational context, you must be ethical and productive. This is exactly the same standard by which an individual should be judged as outlined in the chapter on justice. To be effective, a set of values must be noncontradictory and integrated.

Individuals strongly prefer to work in organizations of which they can be proud. This means they must perceive the organization to be ethical, including the virtue of productivity. One of the critical responsibilities of organizational leaders is to be certain the constituents of the organization can be proud to be associated with it. A common cause of organizational failure is some form of ethical deviation such as dishonesty. This issue is often called reputational risk. By the way, this risk applies to you, your department/area, your organization, and even nations.

One way for an organization, or an individual, to suffer reputational damage (and thereby objectively bring about a reduction in the right to be proud) is to fail to do what it said it was going to do. Overcommitting, including in advertising, can be very destructive. Generally, the best policy, personally and organizationally, is to undercommit and overperform.

For most organizations, productivity toward the accomplishment of the mission is a particularly visible virtue. This is because organizations are typically created for some purpose (whereas individual human beings exist as an end in themselves). Even though productivity is an especially visible virtue, and in for-profit firms often a measurable one, sacrificing other virtues to accomplish short-term productivity goals can be very detrimental. Artificially raising short-term profits through some form of trickery, even if it is legal, will ultimately come back to haunt you.

One self-discipline we tried to impose on ourselves at BB&T was to assume that the world (which in this case includes the media) would know what we did and why we did it. We understood that the media might strongly disagree with what we did and why we did it, but we could be proud of our decisions given our values even in the face of such criticism. During the financial crisis of 2007–2009 it became clear we had made some decisions that had negative outcomes, but we had not made any decisions for which we needed to apologize from an ethical perspective.

At Cato Institute our scholarship and research must be extremely rigorous if we are to have credibility. This is especially true, as libertarian ideals are not the dominant cultural beliefs today. Therefore, our policy recommendations will not typically be consistent with the status quo. It also means our work will be scrutinized often for the purpose of finding (or creating) some error because we are threatening the basic tenets of other organizations and government officials. We cannot afford to make factual mistakes or draw irrational conclusions to prove a point. Thoughtful people will respect our research if it is objective, even if they disagree with the conclusions. The most valuable asset we have at Cato is our brand reputation. It is mandatory that we earn the right to be proud of this brand.

Sometimes humility is defined as a virtue. I have never met a truly humble successful leader. Some high-performing individuals are extremely effective in hiding their pride, but they are proud of what they have accomplished. My observation is that the most impactful leaders are neither humble nor arrogant. The best leaders are objective about their strengths and weaknesses. They have self-confidence based on a rational self-evaluation. Knowing one's weaknesses can enable one to manage the weaknesses more effectively. These leaders are proud of themselves in a quiet way. Real pride is a self-evaluation, not a judgment based on feedback from others. To be genuinely proud of yourself, you must have a clearly defined, noncontradictory value system that is consistent with life on this earth and that you act upon without exception. In other words, to be proud you must have integrity. Once again, an effective value system is integrated.

By the way, pride and integrity are in a special category of virtues in that they are summary concepts. You can have pride because you have other virtues and you have demonstrated integrity with those virtues.

The right to be proud of yourself also is not based on exceptional achievements as seen by others. For example, if someone has achieved great wealth using crony statism instead of real productive work, she does not have the right to be proud of herself (and probably knows it). On the other hand, someone who has a modest income, but has used her capabilities to the fullest and has consistently acted ethically, has the right to be rationally proud of herself.

A CEO who has risen through the organization based on office politics does not have the right to be proud of himself. In addition, this type of individual is likely to be an unsuccessful leader when the test is competitive markets, not the ability to manipulate others.

You have probably heard the saying, "Good guys finish last." This is not true. In the long term, being ethical is also very practical. However, regardless of the economic success or worldly recognition or the lack thereof, virtue is its own reward. Not being virtuous is its own punishment.

11

Self-Esteem (Self-Motivation)

FOR MOST INDIVIDUALS READING THIS BOOK, SELF-ESTEEM IS THE most important issue. When speaking to bright college students at top-tier universities who will be future leaders, I point out that if they fail it will not be because they are not smart enough or well-educated enough to be successful, but almost certainly because of a subconscious self-esteem issue that causes them to act in a self-destructive and/or organizationally destructive manner.

In addition, real self-esteem is the foundation for happiness, and happiness is the goal of life. Hard-work happiness is the Aristotelian sense of a life well lived—flourishing. Businesspeople sometimes get confused. They believe that having money is the goal in life. Money is a good thing. However, money is not an end. It can be a means to an end, but it is not an end. Happiness is the end, and happiness is dependent on genuine self-esteem.

Self-esteem is a complex issue about which much has been written. Let's focus on four critical thoughts about self-esteem.

Self-esteem is based on confidence in your ability to live and be successful given the facts of reality. Therefore, self-esteem must be earned. No one can give you self-esteem. You cannot give anyone self-esteem. You cannot give your children self-esteem; they have to earn it. You cannot give your employees self-esteem; they must earn it.

Promoting children who have not mastered their schoolwork lowers instead of raises their self-esteem.

The primary manner in which you earn self-esteem is by living your life with integrity and living your life consistent with your values. This is why integrity is so important. It is also why having values that are consistent with life and integrated (not contradictory) is essential to the pursuit of happiness—human flourishing.

Introspection can highlight this point. Reflect on the times when you have acted in a way inconsistent with your own principles, typically motivated by a short-term perceived benefit. At some level, you will feel guilty, even if no one else knows what you did and even if you get away with the related action.

This is a psychological feedback mechanism. Because you have developed your principles under the belief that these principles are the morally correct way to live your life, your subconscious sends an alarm when you violate these principles. At least psychologically, you cannot get away with cheating on your own values. There is a price to pay.

The following is the most important concept that will be discussed in this book and the most controversial. Please pay very close attention: **be in focus**.

In order to earn genuine self-esteem, you must believe at a very deep (subconscious) level that you are capable of being a good person and that you have the moral right to be happy. Unfortunately, a very commonly held belief in our society is that as human beings we are born bad. The reason we are bad is because we are born selfish, and selfish is bad.

Visualize Johnny in the sandbox at three or four years old. He is playing with his truck, not bothering anybody. Along comes Fred. Fred would like to play with Johnny's truck. Johnny does not want to give Fred his truck. A discussion/argument ensues. Mom, Dad, Sunday school teacher, or pre-kindergarten teacher intervenes in the argument. Mom says, "Johnny, share your truck with Fred. Don't be selfish. Don't be bad."

There are two great philosophical lessons being taught right there in the sandbox. First, where did Fred get the right to Johnny's truck? This sandbox lesson is the foundation of the modern welfare state. When Johnny and Fred grow up, why should Johnny not have to provide Fred with a four-wheel-drive Ford Ranger? After all, Fred needs (wants) a truck.

What about the lesson for Johnny? And most of the individuals reading this book are Johnny, not Fred. What lesson did you learn? You learned that your life was somehow secondary, not as important as the needs and wants of others. You learned not to fight for what you really want if others need what you have. Somehow, in order not to be bad you have to subordinate your desires to the wants and needs of the Freds of the world.

Let's objectively discuss the concept of being selfish. First, let's define the concept properly as acting in one's rational, long-term self-interest, properly understood. Here's an immutable, nonnegotiable fact of reality: everything that is alive must act in its self-interest or die. A lion must hunt or starve. A deer must run from the hunter or be eaten. Trees shade out other trees to get sunlight. Amoebas take chemicals other amoebas would like to have. Life, by definition, is self-sustaining action. Any living entity that quits sustaining its life dies. This is how Mother Nature designed the system—sorry.

To say that a woman is bad because she acts in her self-interest is the same as saying she is bad because she is alive. If she does not act in her self-interest, she will die.

Let's return to the proper concept of selfish as acting in one's rational, long-term self-interest, properly understood. The reason this definition is important is because we are offered a false alternative—to take advantage of others or to self-sacrifice. Neither of these alternatives is rational, and they certainly are not the only alternatives possible.

Many people define *selfish* as taking advantage of others. In fact, taking advantage of others is not in your self-interest. Taking advantage of others is self-destructive in two contexts. You might fool Tom, Dick, and Harry, but they will tell Sue, Jane, and Bill, and no one will trust you. If you are not trusted, you will not be successful and you will not be able to achieve happiness. I am sure you know individuals whom you view as untrustworthy and manipulative toward their own ends. If possible, avoid such people. If you cannot avoid them, be extremely cautious in your relations with them. If they work for you, discipline them aggressively, and if they refuse to change their behavior, fire them.

There is an even deeper reason why attempting to take advantage of other people is self-destructive. We all want to influence others on some occasions. Leadership is about influencing others. Hopefully, this book will influence you. However, when we let go of reality, when we let go of the truth in order to manipulate others, we do more damage to ourselves than to the person we are attempting to manipulate. Your subconscious knows when you are cheating, and it will undermine your self-esteem accordingly. Probably all of us, at one time or another, have been guilty of some form of attempted manipulation and have paid the psychological price, even if we get the action we hoped would happen. We have lowered our self-esteem.

Because of my career, I have had the opportunity to meet many financially successful people. I have never met anyone who was both successful and happy who achieved these ends by taking advantage of others. I know some individuals who are wealthy who I believe achieved their wealth by manipulating others. These are the most unhappy people I have ever met. Taking advantage of others is not selfish; it is self-destructive.

How about the other alternative—self-sacrifice? Self-sacrifice is the moral code of our society. Whether it is in school, church, or the popular press, we are constantly told to sacrifice ourselves to others, to the less fortunate, creating a very long list of "victims" of all kinds. In fact, anyone who has an income less than 10 percent above the medium income, did not have loving and caring parents, was bullied, was not able to get into a top graduate school, has incurred debt he cannot repay, is a minority and/or female, has poor social skills, is not a good athlete, and so forth, fits into this victim category.

Please ask yourself the following question. *I believe this is the most important question you can ask yourself, and the answer will have a profound impact on the quality of your life:* **"Do I have as much right to my life as anyone else has to theirs?"** Of course, you do! Why would you believe anything else? Why do these others have a right to your life? Of course, you have a right to your life.

Let's pursue this concept at a deeper level. Let's assume *I* do not have a right to my life. Well, humanity is made up entirely of *I*s. Ted is an *I*. Sarah is an *I*. William is an *I*. Eric is an *I*. So if all the *I*s (all the individuals) do not have a right to their life, then no one individual has a right to his or her life. Collectivists/statists see the world through this lens. For the collectivist, individuals do not have rights, only the collective—groups—have rights. Groups practically never have the same basic objectives; therefore, the only way to achieve goals in this collective world is through the use of the threat of force or actual force as embedded in the state.

By not being willing to defend your unequivocal right to your own life, you have supported the idea that no one has a right to his or her own life.

Altruism is another related destructive concept. Altruism is not benevolence. Benevolence is a positive attribute. Altruism is "otherism." It says that everyone else is important but you. Of course, altruism faces the same destructive circular logic in that there are only *you*'s and since no individual *you*'s are important, only the collective, the group, matters; individuals (you) do not matter.

Altruism suffers from an even more philosophically self-defeating problem. Under altruism, if I have more than Tom, I am obligated to give the extra to Tom. However, even though Tom is poor, if he has more than Sally, he is obligated to give the extra to Sally. Even though Sally is very poor, if she has more than Joe, she is obligated to give the extra to Joe, and so forth. However, there are always people in the process of dying. The only way to be equal to someone who is dying is to die yourself.

The point is that when someone gives up her right to herself, she is simultaneously, by logical necessity, arguing no one has a right to his individual life. The collectivist fills this void with an obligation to the collective—society (today), the church (in the Middle Ages), the Fatherland, the Proletariat, [fill in the blank]. Of course, since the collective must be directed by someone, the power hungry fill the void and everyone becomes the vessels of the state with its ability to enforce discipline to achieve the so-called collective good with a gun.

Neither taking advantage of other people nor self-sacrifice are rational alternatives. However, there is a rational and vigorous alternative, which is the moral foundation for individual self-esteem, for organizational optimization, and for a free and prosperous society. The proper ethical perspective is to view ourselves as traders. We trade value for value. Success in life is founded on understanding how to get better together. In the banking business, our goal was to help our clients achieve economic success and financial security, and we expected to make a profit from this trade. A successful person is consistently in the process of finding ways to pursue her ends while helping others achieve their ends through voluntary trades of value for value.

There are only two stable relationship conditions, win-win or lose-lose. Whenever we get greedy and set up a win-lose relationship, our partner gets bitter and we end up in a lose-lose relationship. (Unfortunately, this happens fairly often in spousal relationships.) Interestingly, whenever we get self-sacrificial and create a lose-win relationship, soon we will get bitter and the relationship becomes lose-lose.

In any meaningful relationship, you should ask, "How does this relationship benefit me?" But you should also ask, "How will this relationship benefit the other person?" Because if the relationship is not beneficial to the other person, in the long term it will not be beneficial to you. Finding ways to create win-win relationships is a foundational tool for success and happiness.

And, of course, it is in your self-interest to help the people you care about, who are objectively of value to you—your family, friends, coworkers who share your values, and so on. If you love your children, supporting your children is not a sacrifice, because you love them. In fact, love is the ultimate expression of selfishness. Most people do not think of love in this manner. I use an example with college students to make the point. You are preparing to get married—a major event in your life. Your future spouse comes up to you and says, "I am so excited about marrying you. This is the biggest self-sacrifice I have ever made." Wow! Not exactly what you wanted to hear. Genuine love is very selfish. You want someone because that person is of enormous value to you. He or she is so valuable you are willing to suffer, even risk your life to protect him or her, because without this person your life will lose much of its meaning.

I believe it is in my rational self-interest to support the United Way. The United Way is an umbrella charity organization that performs badly needed support services. I would not like to live in a community without these support services, and I certainly would not want my children to live in a community without them. Therefore, I believe it is in my rational self-interest to support the United Way.

For this reason, I am a consistent and substantive supporter. I do not view supporting the United Way as a sacrifice or a duty. It is a trade—value for value.

There is another misconception about selfishness. The collectivists have, in fact, captured the definition of the concept and changed its original meaning (in the dictionary!) so that many people think of being selfish as being "overly" self-focused. Of course, overly self-focused has a clear negative connotation because *overly* implies an incorrect action. So the collectivists, of all persuasions, have effectively destroyed the original concept of selfish. Clearly, being overly self-focused or self-absorbed is not rational. It is not in your rational self-interest (it is not objectively selfish) to be overly self-absorbed. There are individuals who are overly self-focused and have the equivalent of tunnel vision. They cannot hold the context of the world in which they live. However, this is not selfishness, but simply a type of irrationality.

What would be required for you (or anyone) to act in your rational self-interest properly understood? You would first have to "hold the context"; to ask yourself what kind of world you would like to live in and what you would like to do to create that kind of world. In other words, you would develop a clear purpose. The critical role of purpose has been previously discussed.

Secondly, you would develop a clear set of values and principles by which you will lead your life, values that will promote your success and happiness. Then you would develop strategies to accomplish your purpose. Of course, this is the process we are pursuing in this book.

You would also take care of your body. You would eat properly and exercise appropriately.

You would develop your mind consistent with your intellectual capabilities: read, study, stay mentally active.

You would focus on creating healthy relationships with individuals who share your values. As Aristotle held, friendship is extraordinarily important as a means of self-reflection.

What if everybody had a sense of purpose, rational and life-affirming values, a strategy to accomplish his purpose consistent with his values, took care of his body, exercised his mind, and focused on creating healthy relationships with other people who shared his values? What if everybody acted in her rational, long-term self-interest, properly understood—what if everybody was selfish? The vast majority of the world's problems would be solved in a short period of time.

In the media, in school, and in Sunday school, one constantly hears that the problem with the world is that people are selfish. In my opinion, few people act in their rational self-interest in the context just described. Most people are self-destructive in at least some aspects of their lives. This self-destructiveness is primarily driven by low self-esteem. One of the causes of low self-esteem is the societal reframe that you should be an altruist. However, you cannot be a true altruist and survive. Therefore, for most people the belief they should be altruistic simply is a guilt trip that reduces their self-worth.

I had a family member who drank 24 beers a day. He got cirrhosis of the liver. He continued to drink 24 beers a day. He died. People say he was selfish. He was not selfish. He was self-destructive.

Bernie Madoff embezzled millions of dollars from his family and friends. People say he was selfish. Can you imagine spending 30 years stealing from the people closest to you? Madoff said the best day in his life was the day he got caught. He was not selfish. Madoff was self-destructive.

If you are going to earn a high level of genuine self-esteem, you must believe in your deepest subconscious that you are capable of being good and that you have the moral right to be happy.

Another thought about self-esteem: just as you must judge others, you should judge yourself. Are you who you want to be? Are you moving in the right direction? Are you working toward your purpose? Are you living in a way consistent with your values?

In judging yourself you should use rational standards relative to your natural abilities. For example, I love music, but I do not have any natural musical talents. Should I feel badly about myself because I cannot write a great concerto like Mozart? Of course not. On the other hand, if you have natural abilities that could be used to accomplish your purpose but you have chosen not to develop those abilities, you need to consider this a weakness and develop a strategy to eliminate the weakness.

In self-evaluation (and in creating a purpose), the scale of the goals and accomplishments as judged by the "world" is not important. And the self-evaluation must be relative to your abilities. Maybe you have the ability and motivation to own and operate a single high-quality restaurant. If this accomplishment is challenging and rewarding relative to your abilities and it fulfills your sense of purpose, this is enough.

The most important judgment is your self-assessment relative to your own values and principles. Even if you have not earned a lot of money, but you are living your life consistent with your values, you have the right to a positive self-judgment.

On the other hand, even if you have earned a great deal of money but achieved it through dishonesty or force, you should have a negative self-judgment. The odds are your subconscious will make that negative judgment for you and you will not be truly happy.

There are two possible errors in self-evaluation. One error is to believe you are better than you are. This is arrogance. Ironically, although arrogance often appears as overconfidence, arrogance is typically driven by low self-esteem. Entrepreneurs need a strong sense of self-confidence. However, arrogance can be dangerous, because arrogant individuals overestimate their abilities and underestimate the risk of failure. Self-confidence is very important and has to be earned. Arrogance is fake self-confidence.

The other mistake is to judge yourself as less worthy than you deserve. The individuals reading this book are far more likely to make this mistake than to be arrogant. The nature of relationships with significant people (mom and dad) in our childhood can be a primary driver of negative self-evaluation. We will discuss this issue later. There are several other reasons for this type of mistake. One is an irrational self-performance standard as noted before: "I am not as good of a writer as Victor Hugo, so I am not worthy."

However, underlying most inappropriate negative self-evaluation is a deeper issue. When you were "Johnny" in the sandbox, you learned it was bad to be selfish. However, you are selfish, or you would not be alive. Unfortunately, your subconscious is telling you that you are unworthy because you are alive, because you are selfish.

You are probably deserving of a net positive self-appraisal if you have gotten this far in this book, which is not an easy read. It is not an easy read intellectually, but even more important, it has probably challenged some of your beliefs. And yet you have had the courage to keep reading. If you are already aligned logically and psychologically with the concepts in this book, you certainly deserve a positive self-view. This does not mean you cannot get better, but you should be fair to yourself.

One other thought about self-esteem: the primary drivers of self-esteem for most people are romantic love and productive work. I am not an expert on romantic love. It is probably a survival of the species instinct. However, I will offer one observation. If you are looking for someone to make you happy, you are bound to fail because no one else can make you happy. If you are looking for someone to share your happiness with you, you will almost certainly be successful. Many people would like to share happiness.

For most people reading this book, the primary driver of your self-esteem is your work. You spend a disproportionate amount of your time, energy, and focus at work. Work is used here in a broad context. Properly raising children is very challenging, productive work. Much of your life experience is driven by your work. How you pursue your work (your purpose) drives your self-esteem.

This is something I said to the employees of BB&T on many occasions: "It is very important to BB&T how well you do your job. However, how well you do your job is far more important to you. You might fool me about how well you do your job. You might fool your boss, but you will never fool yourself. If you do not perform your work to the best of your ability, given your level of skill and knowledge, you will lower your self-esteem. Conversely, if you do your work to the best of your ability, given your level of skill and knowledge, you will raise your self-esteem. This is more important than getting a promotion or a raise, because self-esteem is an essential driver of your character."

I tell college students that if they do not do their class work to the best of their ability, they will lower their self-esteem, even if they receive a high grade.

Doing your work well is self-reinforcing. If you do a task effectively, you can become capable of doing a higher-level task. The more you focus on a task, the more competent you become and then the more confident you become. Remember, self-esteem is founded on your self-confidence in your ability to live and be successful given the facts of reality. Achieving mastery in even relatively simple tasks can raise your confidence. Sometimes when you are overwhelmed with a complex task, it is productive to stop, back up, and focus on a simpler task you can master to raise your confidence.

Because rational self-esteem is essential to human well-being, what can organizations do to create a context in which individuals working in the organization can raise their self-esteem?

Here are a few thoughts. Train employees to do the job they are expected to do. The most common reason employees fail is that they are not trained to do their jobs. Some individuals can overcome lack of training. Many cannot. If employees are trained to do a job effectively, they will be more successful, which will raise their self-confidence, which in turn raises their self-esteem, which enables them to do their job better—a virtuous cycle.

After people are trained, create an environment where the employees have the authority to do their job effectively and are simultaneously held accountable for results.

Give employees permission to use their work to pursue their rational self-interest within the context of the organization's mission and values and in the context of creating win-win relationships. More on this subject later in the book.

Of course, there is a connection (integration) with the principles we have discussed. For example, rewarding superior performance (justice) will raise self-esteem and show mediocre performers how to earn more self-esteem.

At the societal level, it is interesting to note that the radical left and the radical right come from exactly the same belief about human nature. They both fundamentally believe that humans are fatally flawed because they are born selfish. The communists and Nazis both attempted to change human nature through educational indoctrination, and both failed.

The modern liberals/progressives are constantly attacking "greed" (selfishness) as the source of economic injustice. According to them, if greed did not exist, we would not have any problems. However, they believe greed exists and only the elitist statist (with a gun) can fix this fatal flaw in human nature.

Modern social conservatives are concerned about the selfish sexual drives of consenting gay adults. Only government force can prevent these selfish actions.

Of course, if humankind is fatally flawed with selfishness, who is there to judge the correct actions? Plato answered this question with the philosopher king, who somehow sees the "real" truth. The statist elitists are the modern equivalents of the philosopher kings. The Founding Fathers had a different response. They said, "Let's not have a king, and let's limit the power of government." They were right.

Being benevolent and acting in your rational self-interest are not in conflict. There are many ways to earn a sense of achievement and accomplishment and in the process raise your self-esteem.

Like a good CEO, let me tell you some stories in this regard. Our first child was born prematurely while we were traveling. My wife stayed in a Ronald McDonald House while our son was in intensive care. Before we went to the Ronald McDonald House, I spent the night trying to sleep in a plastic chair in the hall of the hospital while our child struggled to survive. If you have ever spent the night in a plastic chair in a hospital while your family is in distress, you need no more persuasion that a Ronald McDonald House is a grand, humane idea.

A few years later, my wife and I played a significant role in helping to build a Ronald McDonald House in eastern North Carolina near where we lived. Some of the people involved in the project had stories like ours. Others were just benevolent human beings. Raising the money and being involved in the construction was hard work, but it was also extremely satisfying. Although we did not get paid, helping to build the Ronald McDonald House was productive and meaningful work.

Early in my career, I was asked to join the board of a handicapped workshop. Unfortunately, the workshop had management problems and the board had to become far more involved than is typically necessary. Fortunately, we were able to save the workshop. I found some of the workshop's clients, who were either physically or mentally handicapped, to be very inspirational. They worked hard and intensely relative to their abilities. It was clear that work and self-responsibility were an invigorating experience for them. The best clients did not desire to be dependent—they wanted to work.

I learned a great deal helping build the Ronald McDonald House and helping save the handicapped workshop. Both experiences contributed to my future career in banking, and both were fulfilling.

While helping build BB&T was more challenging and more reward-ing, the Ronald McDonald House and the handicapped workshop were also enriching experiences and in my long-term rational self-interest. I believe all those involved in the projects were benevolent and yet benefited themselves—clearly win-win relationships.

One other aside, all progressive/liberal economists and many con-servative economists talk about the "free-rider" problem. The free-rider problem is supposed to undermine voluntary community proj-ects. The idea is that if the payment for a public (nongovernmental) project is voluntary, some people will not pay and become free rid-ers. This will theoretically keep others from paying and the public (nongovernmental) project will ultimately fail. Obviously, this could happen in theory. However, I have been involved in many nongov-ernmental public projects and have never experienced this as an issue.

The people who build Ronald McDonald Houses and handi-capped workshops do it for themselves. They are not one bit con-cerned that someone might get a free ride on the project. We have a small farm in the mountains of North Carolina. We voluntarily make contributions to our local fire department. I am certainly not going to let my house burn down because someone else is not willing to support the local volunteer fire department. Are you crazy? The free-rider problem is an excuse to use force to accomplish goals that more effectively and efficiently can be achieved through voluntary relationships.

This same type of argument is used to justify the need for govern-ment interference based on so-called market failures. In my 40-year business career, I have never seen a market failure. Any time mar-kets do not work, it is because of the heavy hand (the "gun") of the government. Market failure is another myth to justify expanding government.

Rational self-esteem is essential for individuals and organizations to flourish, and it is also foundational for societal success. The most important societal feature is a culture founded on an individual's right to pursue his or her personal happiness. That culture does not expect individuals to be sacrificed as cannon fodder for the common good, whatever that is. It is also a culture that gives individuals the liberty to pursue their purpose based on their values and beliefs. This is exactly the kind of society envisioned by the American Founding

Fathers. It's a culture that promotes an individual's right to the pursuit of his or her rational self-interest while not violating the rights of others, creating win-win relationships. The individuals voluntarily create communities based on their personal choices, not based on the threat of a gun held by the government.

This type of culture creates an opportunity for individuals to earn rational self-esteem, if they choose to. This creates a self-confident and productive United States of America.

12

Teamwork
(Mutual Supportiveness)

SUCCESSFUL ORGANIZATIONS NEED INDIVIDUALS WHO ARE independent thinkers and have strong personal goals (self-motivated), but much work is accomplished in a team environment. This means that to be successful in most organizational roles, you must be an effective team player. At the organizational level, teamwork is necessary to accomplish complex tasks. In fact, much of leadership is based on the ability to integrate multiple specialists to accomplish complex work that no single specialist could achieve alone.

What is required of an individual to be a good team player? First, you must be committed to the mission and values of the organization. If you do not believe in the mission of the organization or you do not agree with the fundamental values of the organization, you should find another place to work.

Secondly, effective team players do their own job well. Many individuals do not think that performing their job responsibilities effectively is the foundation for productive teamwork. However, in team situations the team is an integrated sum of the work of the individual team members. Fail to perform your work effectively and the team will, of necessity, fail to optimize its performance. A chain is only as strong as its weakest link.

Probably everyone reading this book has been on a team where one individual failed to do his job and it significantly undermined the performance of the team or shifted work to others on the team. It is hard not to be extremely angry with the nonproductive teammate. Being an effective team player requires that you do your job responsibilities well.

The third aspect of effective team players is that they root for their fellow teammates to be successful in a mutually supportive manner. Unfortunately, sometimes we root against our teammates. Why do we do this? Because of that most destructive of all human emotions—envy. Our teammate is outperforming us, and we are threatened in some manner. She will get the prize, and we will not.

There is an old saying in the South: "Lie down with dogs and get up with fleas." In other words, spend time with people who have poor character and it will impact your behavior negatively. The opposite is also true. Spend time with high performers who are also individuals of strong character and the odds are your performance will improve. Seek out individuals who are mentors in terms of results and character, and learn from them.

As you move up the mastery scale, you may have the opportunity to return the favor and become a mentor yourself. In order to teach (mentor) effectively, you must deeply understand the task. Assuming a mentorship role will force you to understand the job at a deeper level so you can communicate the concepts that make for success in this role. The general principle of working to create win-win relationships is clearly applicable in the case of being an effective team player. When you are on a team with someone who is clearly focused on the mission of the team and trying to create win-win relationships, isn't it natural to support that person?

The final aspect of teamwork is not discussed often. Strong team players intellectually reflect on how their individual work impacts the rest of the team and acts to optimize the whole team's performance. As a simple example, a bank branch manager must do her job well. However, she also needs to grasp how her work is impacting the customer service representatives and the tellers in the branch. Is she creating unnecessary work for them, or is she helping them achieve their goals? She needs to reflect on how her work is impacting other departments outside her branch. How is she impacting the "bigger" team? Is she completing the expense voucher appropriately so an employee in the home office does not have to waste time and money redoing her work?

There are a number of benefits from taking the time and focus to understand the organizational impact of your work. First, it can make your job more meaningful. The more relationships you see in your work, the bigger the impact you realize your efforts are achieving. You can simply be putting a bolt on a wheel or you can be helping to build an airplane.

Secondly, the process of practicing how to understand the integration of your work environment versus the accomplishment of tasks will improve your leadership skills. An important part of leadership is integrating the work of specialists. Unfortunately, fairly often when technical experts are promoted to management roles, they fail. They had the capacity to focus on the concrete job responsibilities, but not the ability to see the integrated bigger picture or the ability to assist others in accomplishing the task.

Isn't there a conflict between the pursuit of your rational self-interest and being a team player? One is an individual and the other is a group. There is not a conflict if you fully understand the context. Let's start by discussing the issue of sacrificing for the benefit of the organization. No one should sacrifice, but there are many trade-offs in life. In order to avoid the issue of sacrifice, you need to be clear about your priorities in life and what trade-offs you are willing to make among those priorities.

I would never ask an employee to sacrifice for BB&T, but there were trade-offs. For example, we might offer an employee a significant promotion in a different city where the job opportunity provides an additional benefit because it is potentially a stepping-stone for a future higher-level job. The employee comes to me and indicates she will accept the job, but that it is a significant "sacrifice" because it will dislocate her family. My answer is that if you truly view this new job as a sacrifice, do not accept the offer. If you believe it is a sacrifice, you will expect me to repay you in some way. Also, you may be subconsciously bitter, which will negatively impact your performance and your happiness. I do not want you to make a sacrifice, but there are trade-offs in life. Some of these trade-offs reflect very difficult choices. No one said life was easy. However, the clearer you are about your priorities and the balance among these priorities, the better decisions you will make.

Let's use a basketball team as another example of this concept. The key way to optimize the performance of the team is to ensure that all the players on the team are fully vested in the goal of the team. In this way, any trade-offs (sacrifices) made for the good of the team are consistent with the individual team player's primary objective, which is for the team to win. Suzy is a fairly good shooter, but Tara is better. With 10 seconds left on the clock, Suzy passes to Tara, who is open, even though Tara may be the hero of the game if she makes the shot. However, Suzy's higher goal is for the team to win the national championship.

Of course, an effective coach (leader) attracts team players with a variety of specialized skills (shooter, passer, defender) and understands how to integrate those skills around a common goal. He must convince the individuals that winning the national championship (while obeying the rules) is the ultimate purpose both of the team and the individuals and that the most important contribution this player can make is to play the position that most improves the probability of the team winning. The individual needs to want to win the national championship for herself. In other words, teamwork is a means to accomplish her personal goals. It is a misconception to view the player as just wanting the team to win. She wants to win for herself. Of course, some people put a high value on the relationships of friends on the team. This is just a different standard for rewards. Having her teammates pleased about winning makes her satisfied. The goal is still her happiness.

Many people are not clear about their hierarchy of goals and objectives and, therefore, think they are often forced to make sacrifices, when in fact, they are simply making choices. However, the lack of clarity about their own objectives makes them more likely to make irrational (accidently sacrificial) choices, which at a subconscious level makes them less happy.

One of the most difficult trade-off situations, which can become sacrificial if you are not clear, is work versus family. When is one more important than the other? What trade-offs are you willing to make? The balancing act is magnified when children are involved. You can think of yourself as being on two teams, the work team and the family team. These teams have some overlap, but there are often trade-offs in accomplishing the mission of both teams.

Let me share with you my solution to this issue, which is certainly not given as a general rule. In my case, work is very important to me. I need a sense of purpose, and I have a passion for excellence. My wife and family understand that for me to be happy, work will be a priority. On the other hand, I love my family. The way I handled this trade-off was to plan my calendar as much in advance as possible and to allocate time for vacation and family. I treated these family agreements at the same level or higher than my business agreements. In other words, although I may have allocated more time to business, for the time allocated to family, family was the priority. One of the challenges with families is for all the partners (the adults, especially) to agree with and be clear about the trade-offs. Sometimes partners spend far too little time and energy reaching an agreement on these trade-offs and each partner has a different perspective of the trade-offs. That forces one partner into a real sacrifice, which eventually creates animosity.

One aspect of teamwork with important organizational and societal implications is the voluntary nature of practically all successful teams. When individuals are pushed to join teams, the teams are less likely to be successful than when the participants want to be on the team, even if the team selection is made by someone else.

In an organizational context, you can feel forced to join a team. However, the fact is you can choose not to participate on the team by leaving the organization. This may not be a trade-off you want to make, but it is an option. In society, you can be forced (literally) to participate with your time or money in arrangements in which you would strongly prefer not to be involved.

Libertarians like me are often described as not being team players, that is, not being concerned about family and community, because we are "uncaring rugged individualists." Well, I consider myself a rugged individualist, but my family is one of my highest values, and I care about my community, especially the libertarian community. Being a rugged individualist and loving your family and friends are not mutually exclusive concepts.

Nevertheless, I believe that voluntary relationships are the foundation for friendships and community. Unlike some statists who believe a "village" can be created with the force of government edicts (a "gun") and some social conservatives who think they have the right to prevent individuals from entering into voluntary contractual agreements because of their sexual orientation (gay marriage), libertarians believe that successful communities (teams) are created by voluntary mutual consent. So we value friendship and community, but understand that, like true happiness, friendships and communities are based on individual personal choices and personal responsibility, not the use of force. I personally believe there is a critically important role for charity. However, there is a difference in kind between my choice to give to a charity and a government that will use force to take what I have earned for their ends.

In private organizations, we sometimes pressure people to be on teams. Generally, this is a mistake. Selling them on why the accomplishment of the mission of the team is in their rational long-term self-interest is much more productive. However, in private organizations, we cannot use a gun (or the threat of a gun/jail) to make individuals participate. They can quit.

In society at large, the government has the exclusive authority to use force. Successful teams and communities cannot be built using force.

We have now reviewed the 10 core values used at BB&T and my personal values: reality, reason, independent thinking, productivity, honesty, integrity, justice, pride, self-esteem, and teamwork. Upon reflection, one can see that not only are these values not contradictory but that they are integrated. Failure to execute on one value will make it impossible for you to execute on another value. If you are dishonest, you will be detached from reality, you cannot be rational, you cannot be just, and so forth. Being unjust is an irrational detachment from reality and ensures that you are not an effective team player.

I also argue that this is a comprehensive value system. There are many other positive attributes, but every positive attribute I can think of fits in this system. For example, trustworthiness is a virtue. However, if you are honest, you will be trustworthy. Courage is a positive attribute. But if you have integrity, you will act with courage.

Reflect on our previous discussion of concept formation. Human beings use concepts to integrate a great deal of information. The more information properly included in a concept, the more effective that concept is in helping you to think clearly. If these 10 core values are comprehensive concepts, you can capture the fundamental ethical principles that are necessary to promote your life and your happiness in a few very powerful ideas. By understanding these concepts thoroughly, you will significantly increase the probability of making the right ethical decisions.

Note that although understanding these values is a powerful tool, they are demanding principles. They are not nice-sounding bromides and clichés. Disciplining yourself to the facts of reality can be upsetting when the truth is not how you would like it to be. Dealing with nonperformers as an expression of justice may not be enjoyable. Living these values is not easy, but it is a powerful means to promote your long-term success and happiness—genuine flourishing.

A basic theme of this book is that the principles that are appropriate for individuals are also appropriate for organizations and for society as a whole. Later in the book I will provide a deeper integration of the connection of these 10 core values to societal success and to the principles expressed by the Founding Fathers in the Declaration of Independence and the U.S. Constitution.

TWO

Leading for Personal, Organizational, and Societal Greatness

13

The Role of Emotions

When one highlights rationality, it is often assumed that emotions are not important. There is supposed to be a conflict between reason and emotion. In fact, emotions *are* very important, and there is not a fundamental conflict between reason and emotion.

To be a successful leader you need passion, enthusiasm, and energy. Who wants to follow a passionless, dull, unenergetic leader? Properly aligned emotions can give you intensity and focus and can create resourcefulness. A sense of moral certainty is communicable to others and often energizes their efforts. This is one more reason why it is important to have a set of values that is consistent with life on this earth and one with the other and to act with integrity in accordance with these principles.

Emotions are important, but the nature of emotions and their proper role is often misunderstood. There are some commonsense observations about emotions that are supported by everyday human behavior. Emotions in many ways are similar to primitive values. They are automated subconscious responses mostly developed early in life. Although your emotions evolve throughout your life, the most powerful ones are typically developed when you are young in relation to your parents or early caregivers. But many events in your life can shape your emotions.

For example, perhaps early in your development you met someone you liked and later you met someone else who resembled the original person you liked, and you decided to like that type of person. Or perhaps you did something you did not like and later you did something similar to the event you initially did not like, and you decided you would not like this type of event.

Remember the discussion of concept formation in Chapter 4. You were effectively developing emotional concepts: likes, dislikes, maybes. These emotional concepts were placed in your subconscious and often create automated responses to people and events independent of rational analysis.

It is probable that each of us is born with some emotional propensities. These are tendencies to learn certain emotional lessons from life experiences based on genetic characteristics. However, we do learn our emotions (within the context of these tendencies). This is self-evident in that every individual has a different set of emotions. If our emotions were hardwired genetically, we all would have basically the same emotions because there would be a set of emotions that would improve our ability to survive and perpetuate the species.

If you have multiple children, it is typically observable that from an early age they tend to interpret emotional activities differently, probably reflecting some innate emotional characteristics. Yet you can observe their emotions evolving over time, reflecting the fact that some critical aspects of emotions are learned.

The good news is if you are reading this book it is likely that most of your emotional reactions are helpful. One would not want to have the emotional attributes of the typical criminal. Although your overall emotions may be helpful, I have never met anyone who had perfectly reliable emotions. By that I mean that in all cases your emotions would automatically promote your life and your happiness. If one reflects on how a person's emotions are formed as a child with an especially powerful influence of significant caregivers, it is surprising how functional subconscious emotional programs can be in successful people. My observation is that many people have more functional subconscious emotional programming from a success perspective than a happiness perspective. There are many successful but not particularly happy individuals.

There are several important observations about emotions: First, in a broad context, we have learned our emotions, probably in the context of genetic emotional propensities. Because your emotions are learned, you can change them. I am certain that you can materially change your emotions because I have significantly changed mine. In fact, several members of the BB&T executive management team materially changed their emotions and radically improved their performance. Changing emotions is very difficult. Remember the analogy we discussed in Chapter 5: you are a computer programmer who has been placing programs, including emotional programs, in your subconscious since you were very young. These are the programs that drive most of your emotional reflexes. Changing these programs, these emotions, is painful because it threatens many conclusions you have reached about yourself, others, and the world. Also recall the significance of premises. The subconscious emotional programs are often fundamental premises by which you are living your life. It is scary to objectively examine these premises as an adult. However, if you have a flawed premise, you will necessarily have a flawed conclusion. These emotionally based conclusions can have a profound impact on the quality of your life. For many people, having the courage to rationally examine their emotional premises can be the single most important factor in laying a foundation for the pursuit of their personal happiness.

Changing your subconscious emotional programs requires introspection and courage. There are probably individuals who can achieve this goal without professional assistance, but they are rare. For most people, this type of change requires outside help at least to get started down the path.

In the case of BB&T, we purchased a psychological consulting firm, Farr Associates. All our key managers attended Farr programs, and in the vast majority of cases these experiences improved their performance and increased their job satisfaction and happiness.

As an interesting aside, BB&T became involved with Farr initially based on a recommendation from one of the bank's managers who subsequently confessed to embezzling from the bank. Did he seek out professional help because he knew embezzling was wrong? Did he confess because of what he learned in the psychological training sessions? One thing is certain. He was ultimately happier after he confessed.

Farr works on self-awareness. The goal is to help you understand the subconscious emotional "computer" programs you have written that are directing your life. They accomplish this goal by presenting intellectual models on how you develop your emotions and on how you impact others (and how they affect you) through your behavior. A number of psychological tests and 360-degree-feedback tools are also employed. The most powerful part of the program is the self-awareness exercises. The exercises are presented as guided fantasies and are a form of voluntary self-hypnosis. Practically all significant emotional experiences in our lives are buried in our subconscious and have been used to help write our subconscious computer programs.

You can bring these experiences to consciousness and examine your conclusions as an adult. You will find in a number of cases that the conclusions you drew were irrational as seen from an adult perspective. And yet these emotional premises are driving your life. Because these emotional premises are very powerful and related to many other premises, changing the subconscious program is not easy, but the effort can be extraordinarily valuable. Referring to the computer analogy, this is basic hardwire programming that when changed impacts all your other mental computer programs, so it is hard to change and can take years. However, not changing this basic emotional mental program will keep you from being as successful and happy as you can be.

Let me give you a concrete example from personal experience. In my case, I determined through the Farr process that I had a meta subconscious emotional program that I am "not lovable." And the reason I am "not lovable" is that I am "not good enough." Through voluntary self-hypnosis, I experienced interactions with my mother where I had outstanding school grades (all As and one B) and where she focused, from my view, only on the B. When I dressed or combed my hair, according to my mother, I always looked good, except for . . . [you name the flaw].

Initially, I blamed my mother for the negative emotional connection of these experiences. However, as I reflected back as an adult, her feedback was not inappropriate in the context that from her perspective she was trying to help me improve. Also, her mother, my grandmother, was far more critical of my mother than my mother was of me. Finally, it was blatantly obvious that I was not going to change my mother after the fact, and the problem was not hers, but mine.

Ironically, needing to earn love by becoming good enough is a very powerful incentive and is at least partially responsible for the success I had achieved to that point. However, I was never going to be happy coming from this subconscious emotional premise. Also this subconscious belief caused me to become overly angry when something went wrong; I tended to blame the messenger. I probably will not live long enough to completely rewrite this subconscious emotional program, but I have radically reduced its destructive impact and have still been able to maintain its powerful incentive (or I would not be writing this book).

The goal is to rewrite your emotional programs so that you are happy when you objectively should be happy and you are unhappy when you should be unhappy. When some individuals pursue psychological assistance, their goal is to eliminate unhappiness in their lives. However, there are times when you objectively should be unhappy—bad things happen in Mother Nature. The key goal, however, is to avoid the curse of many successful people, which is to be unhappy when you objectively should be happy. This curse can be a self-reinforcing one in that some individuals believe that this irrational unhappiness is necessary for them to be successful. Not so, as my case illustrates. Also, genuine happiness is a higher value than success. You should not sacrifice your happiness for success. Of course, if you have aligned your values properly and do not have irrational emotional responses, real success and genuine happiness are reinforcing.

The most important concept to grasp is that emotions are not a valid means of knowledge. There is nothing mystical or magical about your emotions. In a certain sense, they are primitive values that you developed largely as a child. To the degree there is a genetic role for them, emotions reflect survival instincts for a world radically different than the world we live in today. These primitive emotional roots are more likely to be destructive than helpful. In fact, the goal should be to train your emotions so they automatically support the conclusions that your rational mind determines.

In any conflict between reason and emotion, always choose reason. Think of emotions as only reason we developed primarily as a child. This idea is especially important for the readers of this book. It is very likely that typically your emotions and your reason are self-reinforcing. When your emotions tell you to act differently than your reason advises, a red flag should be raised. You should carefully reflect on your reason. If upon reflection you think your rational solution is correct, you should act consistently with your reason, even if this decision creates emotional distress.

When speaking to university students, I make this point based on personal experience. When I was in college I faced several decisions where my reason told me to do x and my emotions told me to do y, and I chose to follow my emotions. Forty years later I would like to have those decisions back. Emotions are absolutely not a valid means of knowledge.

Most of the extremely destructive decisions made in business and life are a combination of emotionalism and evasion. The leader rationalizes a decision based on a primitive subconscious emotion and evades the evidence against the decision. The CEOs of large financial institutions that failed were very smart and highly educated; they had been successful in leadership roles for many years. Yet they did not make rational decisions. These decisions were subconsciously driven by primitive emotions such as, "I want my bank to be bigger than your bank" or "if I do not do what other bankers are doing, we will not be able to keep up with the crowd." They then evaded when facts clearly indicated the outcome would be negative.

The two primary culprits who caused the subprime housing bubble that led to the 2007–2009 financial crisis were Congressman Barney Frank and Senator Chris Dodd, the long-term architects of the government's "affordable housing" programs (see my book *The Financial Crisis and the Free Market Cure*, McGraw-Hill, 2013). Both evaded the consequences of their completely irrational support for subprime home lending because they "wanted" subprime lending to work long after the evidence was clear that it would lead to economic failure.

Here is the challenge. Emotionalism (making decisions based on subconscious emotions) can be extraordinarily destructive. However, to be a powerful leader you must be able to express and communicate emotions, because emotions are part of who we are as human beings. The task is to align your emotions with a clear rational purpose executed through a rational value system that is consistent with success and happiness given the facts of reality. When this happens you are entitled to a sense of moral certainty, which will manifest itself as passion and energy in your work. You will naturally become a leader when this happens, because most individuals are not willing to undergo this process. Providing an environment in which the leaders were encouraged and educated on self-awareness was one of the most important strategies underlying BB&T's success.

The role of emotions is critically important for individuals and organizations and equally important to society. This is easy to concretize in destructive decisions by leaders. There are numerous stories of Hitler overriding his generals' advice for emotional reasons that led to military defeats (thank goodness). Firing on Fort Sumter was in the incredibly irrational category given the relative military strength of the North and South at the beginning of the U.S. Civil War. The attack on Pearl Harbor was effectively long-term suicide driven by the arrogance of the Japanese military leadership.

Emotionalism can lead to economic disaster in democracies. The current populism exhibited in Venezuela and Argentina is creating giant economic problems in those countries.

In the United States, recent elections have apparently been driven by emotional reactions to candidates instead of by an understanding of their policies and the probable consequences of those policies. The advice being given to political leaders today is to figure out how to appeal to the emotions of voters instead of how to offer rational policy solutions to tremendous problems such as the looming entitlement financial disaster (including the unfunded liabilities from Social Security and Medicare, which exceed $100 trillion).

Societies tend to have a "sense of life" that reflects a subconscious set of emotional values in a large portion of the population. The United States has had an extraordinarily unique and powerful sense of life from its beginnings. It is an optimistic world view of the land of opportunity, where individuals can achieve extraordinary outcomes and where personal responsibility and individual rights are supreme. It's the land of the free and the brave. This extraordinary sense of life has been under attack from the government education system and many politicians. These cultural leaders offer a different sense of life of the collective good based on duty to others, where egalitarian outcomes represent justice, where elitists are responsible for your life, where envy is a driving emotion, where everyone is entitled to be successful. This is not a new sense of life, but the typical emotional foundation of kings, dictators, fascists, communists, and other statists of all types. "To each according to his ability, to each according to his need" is a very old concept that always requires a wise and powerful king, führer, czar, dictator, and elitist cronies to execute for the so-called common good.

To the degree that this old, destructive sense of life is becoming the standard in the United States and the related destructive emotionalism is driving political leadership selection, we have a serious problem.

The glorification of democracy by both political parties, both at home and abroad, is a form of irrational emotionalism. In fact, democracies have a 100 percent failure rate. The United States is not a democracy. It is a constitutional republic based on the protection of individual rights. U.S. citizens' right to freedom of speech is not subject to majority vote, according to the Constitution. Of course, if you are a business, this right no longer exists. Somehow, for populist reasons, there is supposed to be a difference between commercial speech and civil speech. This is a distinction the Founding Fathers never would have accepted.

Can you imagine trying to run a successful, complex organization where everyone is entitled to equal outcomes regardless of a person's contribution to the results? Would the best leader be selected for the organization based on the emotions of employees where envy was encouraged? How reasonable is it to expect a successful societal outcome using this model?

Emotions matter, and when they are developed rationally they can be a powerful tool for positive outcomes. However, irrational emotionalism combined with evasion destroys individuals, organizations, and societies.

Strategy

THOUSANDS OF BOOKS HAVE BEEN WRITTEN ON STRATEGY. MY GOAL in this chapter is not to cover the subject comprehensively but rather to discuss the integration of vision, purpose, and values with strategy using specifically the BB&T example while connecting to personal strategies and organizational strategies for successful leaders. The points we will be discussing are relevant in the context to all businesses, especially knowledge-driven businesses.

Our beginning point for BB&T (and the appropriate beginning point for almost all organizations) for developing a strategy is the premise that there is only one true natural resource: the human mind. It then follows that competitive advantage is in the minds of your employees, including the ability to take what they know and act on the knowledge in the real world.

At BB&T we created a university to accomplish this objective. Within the university, a systematic training program to develop mastery in critical jobs was developed. To move up the teller hierarchy, one has to have a combination of job experiences and educational qualifications. Completing the process results in certification as a master teller. To become a master customer service representative, the same type of combination of experience and educational attainment is required.

117

In theory, an ambitious individual could enter at the teller level and become CEO of BB&T. In practice, over the years a number of tellers have advanced to become retail lenders and branch managers.

For individuals in the management ranks, there are a series of courses designed to develop leadership skills. It is interesting how many organizations promote individuals from technical jobs to management roles without leadership training. This is a scale issue for small companies, but larger businesses often underinvest in the basics of management training.

There are several aspects of employee education that deserve focus. As CEO, one of my primary objectives for BB&T was to communicate and reinforce the company's mission and values. We prepared quarterly DVDs, which were distributed to employees. Although the DVDs covered operating issues, much of the discussion was on mission and values. I made numerous employee presentations in which the emphasis was on mission and values. Each year, I did a two-hour-long presentation for all employees. The first hour was on strategy and plans. The second hour was focused entirely on mission and values.

In addition, we educated our leadership on economic context by requiring participants in our leadership development program to read *Atlas Shrugged*, *Economics in One Lesson*, and other books on the principles that underlie a free society and free markets.

The goal in educational experiences is to teach the appropriate skills while relating the educational experience to the organization's vision, mission, and values. Every training process is designed to make this integrated connection.

If you have highly trained employees, it would be foolish not to allow them to maximize their contribution because they do not have authority to act. For this reason, at BB&T we operated a very decentralized organization with decision making as close to the client as possible. In order to decentralize, it is critical that employees be trained to make the appropriate decisions. A classic failure is to decentralize without appropriate training. This typically results in poor decision making, which creates a negative reaction that ultimately results in a more centralized bureaucracy.

Obviously, there is a balancing act between authority and knowledge. It is unreasonable to expect a teller to have the knowledge to manage a complex wealth management issue. One aspect of training is to be sure individuals understand the limits of their knowledge. The specifics will vary greatly, depending on the nature of the task. However, the general rule is the farther the decision is from the customer, the less information is available to the decision maker and the less likely the decision maker can consider all the customer's needs.

In this context, one aspect of our organizational structure was to operate with a group of community banks led by a strong community bank president. Each community bank had a high level of decision-making authority relative to the market. This structure recognized that markets are unique and local information powerful. The community banks operated with the same centralized technology and backroom support to reduce cost. The analogy is how the U.S. Constitution envisioned the role of the federal government in relation to the individual states.

Each community bank's performance was objectively evaluated against its goals, against overall organizational standards, and in relation to peers. The community banks had a high level of authority accompanied by a high level of responsibility and accountability.

This decentralized decision-making structure was an important contribution to BB&T's success in weathering the financial crisis without a single quarterly loss. Because decisions were decentralized, the same mistakes were not made everywhere. The banks with centralized risk management make the same errors across the whole organization.

Ironically, the Federal Reserve banking regulators have systematically attacked the decentralized decision-making structure despite its success. A decentralized structure is more difficult for the governmental regulators to control, and control is the goal of the Fed, not risk management. The regulators at the Fed are also trying to force standardization through stress test risk modeling. This process substantially increases the financial system's risk, as all banks will be incentivized to take the same supposedly politically correct risk.

Looking at both of these issues from a societal perspective, if knowledge is essential to individual and organizational success, it certainly is critical to societal well-being. Americans have long been advocates for opportunity based on education. As noted earlier, the U.S. government has radically increased the country's investment in education in real dollars and yet educational attainment is flat. In Chapter 6, the reasons that a government-driven educational monopoly is doomed to failure were outlined. Decentralized education (private for-profit, unregulated education) with resources allocated by market participants is in line with the general organizational principles outlined above.

The decentralization argument presented previously supports the Founding Fathers' ideas that the central government should have "limited and enumerated" powers, with most governmental decisions made at the state or local level. Their ideas for decentralized decision making are consistent with this context.

There are multiple examples of successful management styles, but the management style needs to be consistent with the vision, purpose, and values of the organization. Our management style at BB&T naturally flowed from our principles. The five basic management concepts at BB&T are:

◆ Participative
◆ Team oriented
◆ Fact based
◆ Rational
◆ Objective

Participative management often fails because it becomes a popularity contest. The participative style at BB&T was for the purpose of improving information flow, bringing the correct minds into the decision-making process and obtaining commitment to the execution of the decision. It is critical that participative decision making be disciplined. In the case of BB&T, the discipline was provided by requiring that decisions be fact based, rational, and objective. It does not matter who you are or how many friends you have (although it is good to have friends). The question is whether or not your recommendation is based on the facts, rational, and objective and thereby the best decision given the information available. This mindset minimizes internal politics, which can be organizationally dysfunctional.

At BB&T we took "team oriented" seriously. Many people's attitude toward teamwork was simply that it was an attempt to work together. Although it's necessary for the right attitude toward teamwork to be expressed as a conscious value, as discussed previously, that is not sufficient. Developing effective teams has a scientific component, and the problem must be approached systematically. (I will use *team* and *committee* as synonyms to a large degree for this discussion, although these are different concepts in many situations.) The first step is to be absolutely clear about the purpose and goals of the team. It is interesting how many teams are created in an organization in which the team members do not know the objectives the team is supposed to accomplish or in which team members have different or conflicting objectives. Clarity of purpose always improves outcomes.

Another important factor is determining who is going to be a member of the team. Certainly, the appropriate skill sets among the participants are necessary in order to understand the context for making team-related decisions. However, thinking styles and psychological propensities can play a role. Typically, you do not want every member of the team to think exactly alike. When this happens, which it commonly does, the team will have one or more blind spots. Eventually, the team will be blindsided by a major negative factor that would have been obvious to a team member with a different mindset. When all the team members have the same psychological premises, when they think alike, much of the benefit of teamwork can be lost because groupthink typically prevails.

The size of the team also matters. My own experience is that for many tasks, teams bigger than 10 members can become dysfunctional. Certainly, there are tasks for which larger teams are quite useful. These are typical tasks in which a variety of perspectives is critical and most of the team effort is about information sharing versus decision making. For this reason, corporate boards can be larger than other types of "committees." Despite the perspectives from outsiders, boards are largely about evaluating results and make only a limited number of decisions. Some of these decisions, however, can be extremely important.

Team leadership is critical for a functional team. This is a subset of the general leadership issue we have been discussing. One of the typical challenges for teams is to keep some participants from talking too much and encourage other team members to express their opinions. Unfortunately, sometimes team members with the least

Group Work

to offer talk the most, and those who have valuable insight must be encouraged to speak. One of the most destructive team members is someone who likes to argue for the sake of argument. This person is focused not on reaching a rational decision but on proving he is right. My recommendation is to counsel this type of individual to change his behavior, and if he will not, take him off the team.

If the team is going to be an ongoing entity that has to make important operating decisions on a continuing basis, it can be very productive to use systematic techniques, such as outward bound learning experiences, to help individuals become better team players and to band the team together.

Let me discuss the BB&T executive management team to concretize the team-building process following my election as chairman and CEO. First, all the team members were committed to the vision, purpose, and values of the organization. All were experienced with proven records of success. Most had served in a variety of responsibilities throughout the organization. Practically all had customer contact and sales experience. They understood how the business operated and the revenue-generating process worked. The core team consisted of five individuals who had been through the BB&T management development programs, although individuals were added from mergers as the organization grew. Only one team member (late in my career) was a true outside hire. The core team was significantly above average in intelligence, especially in terms of logical reasoning abilities. All had grown up in modest-income families. All were first-generation college graduates. In fact, three had graduated from a regional university in the top 5 percent of their class. A number had grown up on farms. All the core group had MBAs, but there were other participants on the team who did not have advanced degrees. There was a clear commonality of cultural backgrounds. This commonality could have been a net negative, except for a very strong commitment to logical decision making.

Although the team had cultural cohesiveness, the individual members had very different psychological premises and thinking patterns. Of the five core members, two (including me) were very growth oriented and willing to take risks. Two were far more conservative. One was in the middle of the growth-versus-risk spectrum. A couple of the team members were big-picture thinkers who were

personalities

vulnerable to missing important details. A couple were very focused on "putting all the dots together," with a tendency to add the micros to arrive at the macros. Some were quick to draw conclusions. Others had to analyze very thoroughly.

The psychological propensities in terms of the need for control, achievement, assertiveness, and the like were all in the executive-level categories but varied significantly among the team members. The picture is a team of bright, conscientious individuals with a common cultural background and values but with a wide range of psychological propensities and thinking patterns, all committed to making logical decisions based on the facts.

Every member of executive management attended the Farr self-awareness program described in the previous chapter. After individual attendance, we had Farr facilitate team-building sessions in which we self-disclosed our greatest fears and weaknesses. This is an interesting experience in which you tell people your darkest secrets and everyone says, "So what? We already knew that about you." Of course, the leader of the group gets the brunt of the criticism, which is to be expected.

We also did outward bound–style programs for team building, including ropes courses and river rafting. In fact, we rafted the Chattooga River (fictional name: Cahulawassee River), where the movie *Deliverance* was filmed. Talk about team building! We steered the raft directly into Decapitation Rock. That will wake you up, especially when you fly out of the raft and hit cold water, as a number of the team members did. It was also a very bonding experience.

The purpose of the team determines how much process needs to be employed for team building. However, teamwork needs to be approached intellectually and carefully. To be effective, committees need to be thought of as teams and organized using the same principles.

Our team at BB&T worked because we shared the same core values, and yet we had a variety of strengths and weaknesses that tended to enable us to make better decisions working together than we would have made independently. Groups, teams, and committees do not think. Only individuals think, but a proper team can help individuals think more effectively. Unfortunately, the converse is also true. Teams can sink to the lowest common denominator with the brightest thinker closed out by the decision process. Group thinking is usually the worst thinking.

One way to fight groupthink is to have decentralized yet integrated decision making. We were conceptually organized as a group of overlapping circles (see Figure 14-1), which created much better information flow and more integrated outcome responsibilities.

One clear tendency in organizations is for power to be drawn to the home office. To fight this tendency, we created a Community *CDs* Bank Presidents' Council, which had approval authority over any operational and marketing decisions that had customer impact. The home office support staff complained endlessly about having to go through this process, but it helped to keep the authority in the organization decentralized. The rule was that there had to be a consensus among the community bank presidents, usually represented by support of at least 75 percent, for a client-related process or marketing change to move forward. Once the decision was made, even the dissenting community bank presidents had to execute the agreed-upon strategy with enthusiasm. In other words, all participants had an

FIGURE 14-1 Participative Organizational Structure

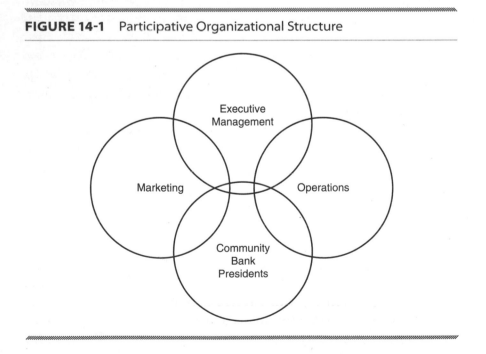

opportunity to express their opinions and try to influence the decision, but once the decision was made, they had to be with the team.

Strategic planning was an important element of participative management at BB&T. We had a top-down, bottom-up planning process. The executive management team twice a year had off-site strategic planning sessions—one for three days, the other for one week. We would create a big-picture plan, which became the context for the bottom-up planning. Oftentimes when our big-picture plan met the reality of the bottom-up plan, it resulted in debate and compromise. We had strategic plans for every department and every branch. Every employee had a personal performance and development plan.

In our executive management strategic planning sessions, while I facilitated the meetings, one of the rules was that we were all equal in terms of input into the planning process. This context allowed me to express my opinions without silencing other views. One comment I always made to start the meeting was that I was not interested in argument for argument's sake; however, I also was not interested in agreement for the sake of agreement. Frankly, anyone who was going to knee-jerk agree with me is useless. I typically agree with myself.

On controversial issues, we always voted the question with me voting last. I reserved the right to overturn the majority vote. However, in almost 20 years as CEO, I overturned the majority vote only three times. Fortunately, I was right all three times. On the other hand, I was in the minority on a number of decisions, and the majority decisions proved to be correct.

This is how participative management can be effectively implemented. It is not like majority voting in the political process, where most people are ignorant of the issues and vote on name recognition or for other superficial reasons. The participants in the executive management team are intelligent, knowledgeable, competent, and qualified in every way.

You do not always have the luxury of working on teams with shared values and that are made up of first-class individuals. In those cases, participative management is more about gathering information and creating consensus, with directed decisions sometimes necessary.

To reiterate, participative management can be very destructive if it becomes a popularity contest, driven by internal politics, and/or if it results in groupthink. It is critical to discipline the leadership process by making decisions based on the facts, which are rational and objective. Leading in a participative management environment is far more difficult than authoritative leadership because it requires persuasion and integration. Being tyrannical like Captain Bligh of the HMS *Bounty* is easy until your ship hits the rocks because your crew is afraid to give you feedback. Participative management is the most difficult leadership style to execute, but it also has the best results over the long term. This is because there is more information in the system and more differing perspectives and better execution when individuals are involved in the decision-making process. Authoritarian organizations can be successful for a while, but they almost always fail in the end if they develop any scale because of the lack of information flow to the top of the organization.

BB&T acquired a number of companies that had authoritarian leadership styles. It took several years for the leaders (some of whom left) and the employees to grasp the participative leadership process. When they understood the process, however, they were happier and results improved.

BB&T operated with a management concept that flowed inevitably from its value system and was integrated with the management style just discussed. This management concept was to do the following:

- Hire excellent people.
- Train them well.
- Give them an appropriate level of authority and responsibility.
- Expect a high level of achievement.
- Reward their performance.

BB&T's goal was to operate a highly autonomous, entrepreneurial organization. To make this concept effective required very competent individuals who were well versed in BB&T's philosophy and masters of their field of endeavors.

This allowed us to have much less expensive control systems and to be much more responsive to customer needs. Typically, the argument for centralization is that it is efficient. There are certainly some activities that are more efficient when centralized. But in many cases the actual motivation for centralization is control. My experience is that while there is a significant need for accountability, the most effective control is highly trained employees who are committed to a rational value system. Despite being decentralized and serving many rural markets that are less concentrated, BB&T was in the top 5 percent of banks in its size category in efficiency. We simply spent substantially less on control systems than our competitors.

As might be expected, I am working on using these same concepts at the Cato Institute. My predecessor at Cato, Ed Crane, built the organization from scratch and did an amazing job of creating a world-class libertarian think tank. However, Ed had his own leadership style and a tremendous amount of information in his head. In addition, the organization has grown significantly, and it is time to scale up from a single, dominant decision maker to allow Cato to continue to grow.

One of our first steps toward growth was to conduct a strategic planning session. As you might imagine, this was an interesting experience for a group of libertarian, individualist free thinkers. There were several participants in the planning process who were opposed to strategic planning in principle. Fortunately, we ended up with an excellent plan that is in the execution process.

We have created an executive management team using the same principles outlined previously. We are on a learning curve, but the foundation for a successful team has been laid. We also developed a goal-setting and performance evaluation system that is in the first year of implementation.

The early results from this approach are encouraging. Cato experienced a substantial increase in revenues, record production of output (articles, media interviews, and the like), and substantial impact in several policy areas. We were able to retain practically all our key policy scholars despite the cultural change. We are extremely fortunate to have an outstanding group of individual employees, board members, and sponsors who are passionately committed to Cato's mission.

Hire fundamentally good people, train them well, give them authority and hold them responsible, expect them to be successful, and reward their performance. Would you like to work for an organization that consciously holds these principles? Many of the best people do.

Integrating Strategy and Process (Total Quality Management/Six Sigma)

THIS CHAPTER FOCUSES ON THE RELATIONSHIP OF STRATEGY TO process. One of the more fundamental strategic decisions an organization must make is its customer value proposition. Value (V) in this context is the relationship of quality (Q) to price (P): $V = Q/P$. The higher the quality relative to the price, the greater the value from a customer perspective. For this purpose, quality, price, and value are all as seen from the customer's perspective.

Many businesses offer a range of value propositions designed to serve various customer segments, such as General Motors (GM) does with Chevrolet versus Buick versus Cadillac. Maintaining the value proposition relative to customer expectations is critical to brand success. For example, at one time GM allowed Cadillac's quality to deteriorate, which then threatened the value of its brand.

There are customer segments across the value proposition scale. Typically, acting consistent with your value proposition is fundamental to long-term success. Walmart has always had the best prices.

When it attempted to upscale on quality and raise prices, it met significant customer resistance.

Usually it is not practical for a brand to have more than one value proposition, although one company can offer a variety of value propositions by using multiple brands, such as GM does.

It is extraordinarily important that all processes in the organization be aligned to deliver the value proposition that the customer expects. Failure to deliver can quickly destroy a brand.

Determining where your organization should operate on the value proposition scale, whether the focus should be on high quality or low price, is critical to success. The goal is to deliver greater value at lower cost as seen through the customers' eyes. This can be an important issue in managing an internal function. You need to understand the value proposition of your internal customers and the relationship to the value proposition of the ultimate client.

In establishing a value proposition, an organization needs to understand the competitive landscape and its own strengths and weaknesses. What value propositions are being filled, and where are their opportunities?

Again, let me concretize this concept and its execution using BB&T as an example. We consciously decided to be a quality-driven organization. We realized that price always matters. However, our concept was to deliver the best value proposition by focusing on quality while remaining price competitive. In a low-margin business such as banking, we tried to deliver a ½ percent more value and charged a ¼ percent higher price.

Why choose quality over price? Banking is a very personal business. The quality of financial advice can have a profound impact on the quality of your life. Quality is particularly important for individuals who have money or borrow large amounts of money. The vast majority of profit in the industry is with these quality-focused client segments. Also, BB&T did not have a natural price advantage. We initially operated in rural markets and did not have scale relative to the dominant competitors. In addition, we believed that our unique focus on purpose, ethics, and education/knowledge would allow us to significantly differentiate our quality from our primary competitors. Much additional analysis can go into determining your value proposition, but this highlights the major issues.

Once a value proposition is determined, the organization's fundamental focus must be committed to delivering the value proposition that will drive the brand. If you decide to be a price-driven competitor, the defining question is how do you cut your cost so the organization can afford to offer lower prices? Walmart "invented" importing in scale from China, bringing a tremendous benefit to lower-income consumers in the United States.

If quality is the focus, the question is how to differentiate quality within an acceptable price range. At BB&T we determined the quality drivers from a client perspective for banking services, which are:

- Reliability
- Responsiveness
- Empathy
- Competence

People want to have a banking relationship with individuals and an organization that they can trust to be reliable. They want answers in a responsive manner, even if the answer is no. Human beings prefer to do business with someone who treats them as a unique, special individual, not as a number. Also, clients want to obtain services from people and institutions that are experts. It is fine that your doctor has a friendly bedside manner, but it is critically important that he know how to treat your health issue.

If you reflect on the principles we have discussed previously, they are the foundation of quality client service. In this context, our mantra was that we will absolutely never, ever take advantage of anyone, nor do we want to do business with those who would take advantage of us. Our partners are long-term relationships and should be treated accordingly. We are committed to creating win-win partnerships. One attribute of partnerships is that both partners must keep their agreements. We keep our agreements. The goal is always to try to find opportunities to get better together.

But it takes more. To be reliable, an organization must have a clear set of policies that it adheres to at all times. One of BB&T's traditional strengths was to do our best to help clients through difficult financial times. Tragically, during the financial crisis of 2007–2009, BB&T was forced by banking regulations to put small businesses out of business that we traditionally would have found a way to keep in business. Sadly, this was an unavoidable violation of the long-term value proposition.

In order to be responsive, employees must be empowered to make decisions. Decentralized decision making supports responsiveness. Employee education is fundamental to high-quality service. They must have the technical skills to fulfill their responsibilities. They must have the context to know when to refer customers to other employees who can better answer the customers' questions. Education and knowledge create confidence, which allows employees to treat the clients in a more empathetic manner, to be more responsive, and to be more reliable. At BB&T, one of the most important strategic decisions we made early on was to choose to invest significantly more in employee education than our competitors. We substantially reduced our advertising budget and increased our educational investment.

The theory was to grow our business through word of mouth. If we had better-educated employees who were committed to helping our customers, then our satisfied customers would refer their friends to BB&T. The strategy worked.

Clearly defined and carefully developed processes can impact service quality. We trained our employees on superior service quality from both an attitude and action perspective and then inspected the behaviors. Employees were trained to answer the phone in three rings or less with a scripted information message; for example: "Thank you for calling BB&T. This is John Allison. How may I help you?" Customer service representatives were educated to always shake the client's hand and always thank her for her business. Tellers were to always say the client's name and thank him for his business. And so forth. Once these behaviors have been internalized and become automated, employees do not have to think about the behavior, and their minds are free to focus on the clients' needs.

One core area to automate behavior is when clients are upset about a service issue. It is critically important to let the clients know you can understand why they are upset and you are empathetic to their concern. This is true whether or not it is the client's mistake or the organization's error. Clients need to know you hear them—that you are listening. Once this emotional connection is made, you can move to actual problem solving. If it is an organizational mistake (or if the clients reasonably believe it is the organization's mistake, not their own), a token of atonement as a symbol of apology by the organization is appropriate. Client loyalty can be deeply strengthened or destroyed by how complaints are handled. Complaint resolution needs to be instilled by training and systematized. Again, one objective of systematic training is to create automated responses to the basics with the goal of freeing the employees' minds to intellectually deal with the concrete issues of the clients. The systematic behavior cannot be an excuse for the employees not to think.

One fundamental role of management is to inspect what you expect. Because of the importance of quality-differentiated behavior to BB&T's success, quality measurements were typically part of all client contact and many internal departments' incentive programs. In the branch, quality was measured based on client satisfaction surveys and on the results of anonymous "shops" by bank-trained service specialists. For client contact roles, experienced employees were expected to get 100 percent on the service shop and would be rewarded accordingly. Our community banks were rated on service quality and ranked against one another on results. Community bank presidents' incentives were partly driven by these service quality statistics.

We also measured ourselves against competitor organizations. Our service quality was consistently better than our competitors', which resulted in lower client turnover and a much higher willingness of our clients to recommend BB&T to their friends.

Internal service quality can also be systematized. One classic mistake is for internal departments to misjudge what is significant to internal customers. Departments create self-reinforcing feedback based on their assumptions of what is important to their internal clients.

We used internal service agreements to significantly improve quality and reduce cost. These agreements begin with the internal clients being extremely clear on what they needed to perform their work efficiently and effectively from their internal service provider and what they were willing to "pay" to achieve this service standard. Oftentimes the internal clients' priorities were radically different from those of the department providing service even though the service department had the best intentions. The department was unaware of the real needs of its "customers" and was driven by its misconceptions.

The service department is measured by its execution of the service agreement. If it achieves or exceeds the service standard and reduces cost, a portion of the savings turns into an incentive for employees in the service department. We were able to achieve significant savings and improve quality by ensuring alignment of goals through integration of activities.

So one of our core strategies was to be a quality-differentiated competitor. Implementation of this strategy required integration on a number of important substrategies. First, our philosophy was based on creating win-win relationships in the context of making the world a better place to live. Secondly, because we were fundamentally individualist, it was appropriate that we treat our employees and our clients as thinking, special, and unique individuals. To develop competent service, it was essential that employees be trained to have a service attitude and have and possess skills and knowledge to solve the clients' problems and needs; hence, an investment was made in employee education. In addition, it was crucial that employees have the authority to make decisions within their skill set and be held accountable for the outcomes.

A process that creates automated behavior can free the employees' minds to deal with a specific situation using their critical thinking. It is essential to remember the process is not the end, but a tool to be used for better customer service. When the process becomes the end, the organization becomes a bureaucracy like a government agency. "Inspect what you expect," or you will not be taken seriously. Reward for delivery of the quality proposition—and punish for failure to deliver.

The vast majority of employees want to deliver superior service quality to their customers, including internal organizations. Creating an environment where they can achieve this end improves service quality and employee morale, which improves service quality, and so forth. When attempting to predict how good the quality of service will be from an organization, many clients look at how satisfied the employees are with that organization. If employees are treated poorly, why would clients expect to be treated well?

Note the integration of a variety of activities toward a primary strategic objective. These activities may not necessarily be seen as integrated, but they are. In addition, it's critical to keep the context (in this case, superior client service) in mind. The parts of the strategy are only meaningful and helpful in the context of the goal of the strategy.

In the early 1990s, BB&T began implementation of a Total Quality Management (TQM) process, which eventually evolved into a Six Sigma program. There have been numerous books and articles written on TQM and Six Sigma. My objective here is not to cover these programs but to give you an overview of their objectives. The fundamental idea behind Total Quality Management is that systems and processes drive outcomes. The concern is that management tends to attribute too much of the outcome of a system or process to the performance of the individuals within the system. In that case individuals may be unjustly criticized or unjustly rewarded when the system design is driving the results versus the behavior of individual participants in the system. Also, changing the behavior of individual participants or changing who participates in the system (by hiring or firing) will not change the outcome. The way to change the outcome is to change the system design itself.

As a simple example, if you are a waiter responsible for toasting bread and your toaster (the system) is hardwired to burn the bread, no matter how good of a job you do scraping the burned part off the bread, you are not likely to have satisfied customers. Improving your bread-scraping skills is not going to materially impact the outcome. A manager replacing the waiter with a better, faster bread scraper will not impact the results materially. Obviously, the toaster (the system) needs to be replaced. The system (the toaster) is driving the outcome.

The related lesson is that trying to fix quality mistakes is much less efficient than redesigning the system so it does not make quality errors. Build quality into the system. Quality is a combination of attitude and process. These are reinforcing phenomena. The waiter in the previous example is working with a defunct system and simultaneously being punished (with smaller or no tips) and will not long have a positive attitude. We sometimes design systems that make it practically impossible for employees to deliver the quality to their clients that we demand they deliver.

The toaster example is simple, but the principle is replicated throughout organizations in which systems drive outcomes. Managers often fail to reflect on what behavior the system is incenting or effectively forcing the employee to exhibit. Many times focusing on the systems design is far more productive than focusing on the behavior of individual employees.

This concept, while very useful, can be carried to an extreme and become counterproductive. In a properly designed system, individual behavior can vary significantly and greatly impact the quality and quantity of the system's outcome. As another example, in the banking industry until relatively recently the dollar amount of a check had to be input into a proofing machine manually. Some individuals have an incredible talent to perform proofing (reading and inputting the dollar amount of the check) at great speed and with few errors. (I am not one of those individuals.) The difference in both quality and quantity between proof operators was very material, within the same system. The high-performing proof operators deserved to be better paid. Of course, the real improvement in production was creating machines that could read the amount and related data on the check and effectively eliminated the proof job. Knowing whether the system or the individual is driving the outcome is an important role for management. Improving systems (innovating) typically has the greatest impact on outcomes, but many times we do not know how to improve the system. In these cases, individual performance is critical.

Also in numerous cases (especially related to personal service) the system reflects broader principles (not the mechanical-type system, which is typical of manufacturing) in which the individual's ability to intelligently apply a principle (hold the context) while adjusting to the specifics of the circumstances is critical to the outcome. In these cases, mechanically applying the system can be very destructive. Sales and service based on personal relationships fit in this category. In this case, performance can be improved by coaching the right behaviors, but the employees must be able to customize their actions to the circumstances of the specific situation. Mechanical behavior, driven by a system, will not work in these settings.

Another important aspect of TQM is differentiating between special causes and expected systems outcomes. Special causes are

Enron

unusual events that cause unexpected outcomes. If you redesign the system because of the special events, you will make the system less efficient. For special events, deal with the event. If the system's typical outcome is outside the acceptable range, however, the system needs to be redesigned.

Unfortunately, a large portion of government policy is driven by misidentification of special causes from a systems design perspective. The Sarbanes-Oxley Act of 2002 is a classical example of this type of legislation. There were several large accounting fraud-related failures. WorldCom and Enron were the most visible, which received a great deal of publicity. These visible frauds were the motivation for the Sarbanes-Oxley legislation, and yet they were clearly special cases, not a systems problem. Fraud has been against the law since the Roman Empire, at least. These firms cheated the accounting system, and the culprits were caught and prosecuted.

On the tenth anniversary of Sarbanes-Oxley, I had the opportunity to debate Senator Paul Sarbanes. Because my 40-year career in banking has been primarily focused on risk management, I did some research on actual fraud-related losses. Interestingly, fraud-related losses have increased significantly since the implementation of Sarbanes-Oxley. This may be related to the economy, but it is also partly related to the fact that fewer firms have chosen to become public. The process of executing a public offering and the capital raised in a public offering reduce fraud-related losses. By reducing the frequency of public offerings, Sarbanes-Oxley increased fraud losses. Of course, many of these losses were incurred outside of public markets, but from the perspective of the economy, a fraud loss is a fraud loss. (I won the debate, based on objective measurement.)

Unfortunately, Sarbanes-Oxley has increased accounting costs significantly, with negative benefits to the economy. But it has been a major revenue source for the accounting industry. Therefore, members of the accounting industry will resist any changes to the law because they have a vested interest in its continuation.

In the United States we are educating far more accountants and thereby fewer engineers and computer programmers than we would have if Sarbanes-Oxley had never become law. This reduces our overall productivity.

Tragically, much of modern regulation is based on this same conceptual error wherein a small number of visible examples drive government regulations, which reduces the overall productivity in an industry; thereby, the standard of living is lowered for all of us.

Conceptually, one can view rule of law as a system. The system should not be redesigned because of random events (special causes), especially if the system has been operating effectively for hundreds of years.

Cato scholar Bruce Yandle and his grandson Adam Smith have recently published a book, *Bootleggers & Baptists*. It outlines a general principle that results in destructive policy. As an example, in the mountains of North Carolina, it was illegal to sell alcohol. (It is illegal even to this day in some counties.) But it was easy to buy homemade alcohol (moonshine) from bootleggers. The anti-alcohol laws prevailed despite their lack of effectiveness and negative impact. (Bootlegged alcohol can blind you.) The Baptist preachers supported keeping the sale of alcohol illegal for moral reasons. The bootleggers gave to the Baptist church so the preachers would get out the anti-alcohol vote.

The massive subsidies to ethanol are a result of the same process. The environmentalists on the left support renewable energy. The corn farmers know that corn prices will be substantially higher if ethanol production is subsidized. Despite the fact that it is now clear that ethanol is more environmentally destructive than fossil fuels, as shown by Princeton's Timothy Searchinger and others in a 2008 article published in *Science*, the subsidies continue because of an embedded lobbying effort.

By the way, some environmentalists must be very naive. My early career was as a farm lender. Some of the chemicals used to grow corn have a skull and crossbones on their labels, because if you drink them you will die. They are unlikely to improve the environment.

Both individual behavior and system design drive outcomes. The goal is to design systems to produce optimal outcomes, which often requires that the system incentivize high levels of performance by the individuals in the system. In the context of properly designed systems, individual behavior can vary widely, and high performers should be rewarded to produce optimal results.

The law is a system. Poorly designed legal regulations, especially those based on a fundamental lack of understanding of special causes or those created for political motivations, produce negative results. Unfortunately, many regulations incentivize very nonproductive behavior in individuals. Often regulations look like the defective toaster described previously.

16

Rational Optimism (Passion and a Positive Attitude)

AS HUMAN BEINGS, IF WE CHOOSE TO BUILD ON THE FACTS OF reality and our ability to reason, we are capable of achieving both success and happiness. Realism does not mean pessimism. Because our goals are based on and consistent with reality, we are fully capable of accomplishing them.

Believing you can accomplish a goal does not ensure you will do so. However, believing you will not accomplish a goal almost ensures that you will fail.

An appropriate way to view goal setting is as a rational optimist. A rational optimist does not set goals that are practically unachievable. Instead, she sets challenging (optimistic) but achievable goals. "Reach" goals incent a higher level of motivation. Easy goals can disincent high-performance results. For example, if the so-called experts believe 8 percent growth is possible, you should strive for 10 percent growth. The higher but not impossibly attainable goal will motivate you to work harder and to be innovative. Even if you do not reach the goal, you will very likely achieve more than you would have with a lower goal, and you will learn more in your efforts to achieve the higher performance. This reach-based learning will enable you to accomplish a higher level of performance next year.

In school, there are students who have a subconscious expectation of making a B grade. When they make an A on a test, they do not study for the next test and then make a C, creating a B average. Their expectation limits their outcomes. Do you ever limit yourself in a similar manner? Are you afraid to be too successful?

On the other hand, having irrational, overoptimistic expectations can also destroy motivation and/or cause behavior that is destructive in the long term. CEOs sometimes set goals for their organizations that are not rational given the nature of their business. These types of goals can demoralize employees because they are impossible. Trying to achieve the impossible is not typically motivating over the long term.

In addition, unrealistically aggressive goals can cause individuals and organizations to make short-term decisions that reduce long-term effectiveness. Classic examples in business are to underinvest, cut costs excessively, or to take too much risk.

Ironically, success can breed irrational optimism. In my banking career, there were a number of financial institutions that were number one performers for several years. They tried to sustain this performance when the factors that had driven their outsized performance changed. They attempted to outrun the inevitable by excessive cost cutting and excessive risk taking, which ultimately created serious performance problems.

Deciding what kind of performance goals to set is critical to achieving the most productive goals. During my tenure as CEO of BB&T, the bank grew at a 20 percent compound growth rate for 20 years. It's telling that there was not a single year where we set a goal in advance to grow 20 percent or more. Our goals were focused on world-class execution of the philosophy, strategy, and processes discussed previously. We were simultaneously committed to always looking for opportunities and to relentless commitment to process improvement. Our typical growth goals were 8 to 10 percent, and these growth goals were far secondary to quality goals. The quality goals were rationally optimistic—world-class performance.

Rational optimism begins with objective assessments of the range of possible outcomes and commitments to the high end of the objectively defined range. Obviously, for most objectives setting goals is part art and part science. In many areas, however, the range of rational outcomes is knowable. The compound difference between 6 percent and 8 percent over 10 years is material. The compound self-esteem impact of working to your potential day in and day out is significant.

Are your life goals below your potential? Or are your life goals pipe dreams? One indication of pipe-dream goals is your consistent choice not to pursue the goal. You have always wanted to have a PhD in philosophy. However, despite having graduated from college 10 years ago you have never taken a master's-level philosophy course . . . and you probably never will. This may be a sign that you should either pursue this goal or let it go. Holding the goal may be keeping you from pursuing goals more suited to your talents and motivations.

Having rationally optimistic goals and working toward the achievement of those goals is essential to the pursuit of individual happiness and organizational success.

Should countries have goals? No and yes. Most of the goals that are described by political leaders are based on an assumption that the country is one monolithic whole. In reality a country is millions of individuals with wildly varying goals. When political leaders talk about goals for a country, they are planning to use force to make individuals comply with the goals of others. This is true whether or not the country's goals are held by the majority of people in the country.

Because governments are by definition able to use force, there is only one goal that is legitimate for a government—to protect individual rights; in other words, to prevent the use of force by one individual or group against another individual or group. The legitimate goal of the U.S. government (or any proper government) is to protect, as expressed in the Declaration of Independence, an individual's right to life, liberty, and the pursuit of happiness. Government does, therefore, need a goal, but the goal is clearly delimited, as government has the power of force, of the gun. Individuals and organizations do not have the right to use force to make others comply with their goals. Therefore, there is a difference in kind between government goals and individual/organizational goals, which are fundamentally voluntary.

The concept of rational optimism is based on the more general concept of a benevolent universe. The benevolent universe idea does not imply that Mother Nature is nice. In fact, Mother Nature is demanding and mercilessly adheres to the laws of reality. In this context, Mother Nature is neither mean nor benevolent, she just is. The benevolent universe concept is that given the nature of reality (Mother Nature), human beings have the ability to survive and prosper—to flourish. We are not guaranteed success in our pursuits, but we are capable of success.

Based on your world view, this capacity may be the result of divine design or evolution. Either way, we humans are not destined to have unhappy lives and die young. We have the capacity to create good lives for ourselves. Humans have the capacity for success and happiness—we can flourish.

Reality (Mother Nature) is not easy to master, but she can be mastered. If you view yourself as doomed by destiny to have an unhappy life, you will have an unhappy life. Realizing that you are capable of living a meaningful life significantly increases the odds of your living a meaningful life, but nothing can guarantee success.

To some degree, countries have a more or less benevolent world view embedded in their culture. The United States traditionally has had an extraordinarily positive benevolent universe world view as an aspect of the American sense of life. Statist movements (including the current progressive movement) have a very malevolent view of life. Statists view humans, in general, as flawed, selfish, and destructive. It is only the wise few, the elitist philosophers, who can keep us from destruction. Plato was the original architect of this idea in the philosopher king concept. This idea has, in fact, dominated much of human history and is a major impediment to human progress.

The United States was the first and is the only country founded on the idea that if freed from the shackles of force (by government or mobs), humankind is naturally able to not only survive but prosper. Man is enlightened.

Those who argue that America is not special are ignorant of human history or dishonest or have a deep malevolent sense of life. Sense of life is a much deeper issue than power lusting or arrogance. This negative sense of life is antihuman at its very roots.

When you hear a politician, a statist, an academic, an environmentalist, or a religious zealot present an argument from this malevolent universe viewpoint, watch out. You are in the presence of a very destructive idea.

Relating back to the individual and organizational level, it is critical to maintain a positive attitude in the face of adversity. Maintaining a positive attitude should not reflect a lack of attachment to reality. In fact, if you appear not to accept that the situation is negative, your team will not have confidence in you. For self-leadership, not consciously admitting the negative situation is a form of destructive evasion. The proper attitude is to consciously and openly define the negative situation, while proposing a rationally optimistic solution. In business, this sometimes means that you keep smiling and telling the team to focus when you personally are petrified. Whatever the odds of success, maintaining a rationally positive attitude, while objectively evaluating the facts, improves the probability of a better outcome. If the leader of the team becomes convinced that failure is inevitable, failure probably is inevitable. Having positive energy improves focus, which often improves results.

Earlier we discussed the need for emotional passion in leadership (including self-leadership). Under adversity, the need for passion increases. A tool that is often helpful is to go back to basic premises and your (or the organization's) purpose. If our work is important, then the obstacles are worth overcoming.

Also, if you have acted with integrity and still the outcome is negative, there is no reason to apologize. The deep downer occurs when you know the negative results are caused by your failure to live in integrity with your fundamental principles.

To be rationally optimistic, you must have a clear conscience. We all make mistakes. Even well-intentioned actions that are reasonably well thought out can have negative consequences. Forgiving yourself for even these types of mistakes can be difficult if the outcome is materially destructive. Nevertheless, it is much harder to forgive mistakes that were the result of violating your values. In those cases, to justify forgiving yourself you must admit the real reason for this transgression and deeply commit not to make the mistake again.

Unfortunately, many people use guilt as crutches to forgive themselves without genuinely committing not to make the error again.

Because they feel bad (guilty), they have paid for the transgression. At the subconscious level, this becomes permission to make the mistake again. They then get to feel guilty again and so forth. Operating from guilt makes it almost impossible to maintain a positive attitude. Being guilty is typically destructive. You should admit your mistake to yourself and others, apologize, make restitution (if appropriate), and move on. Watch employees who use their remorse, from guilt, to ask forgiveness. Forgiveness requires more than remorse.

Rational optimism is not a detachment from reality, but it is reflective of a can-do attitude. Being rationally optimistic requires a clean conscience. If you are driven by guilt, you cannot be a rational optimist. Being rationally optimistic increases the probability of success.

The United States is the only country in history defined by a rationally optimistic sense of life. As statism continues to erode liberty, optimism naturally declines, because being in control of your life, being free, creates a natural sense of opportunity. When the average person in a culture has a rationally optimistic sense of life, the probability the society will be successful increases significantly.

17

Beliefs + Behaviors = Results

In trying to improve outcome, many managers focus on results. Focusing on results is largely a useless exercise, as the results being obtained are to be expected based on how individuals are acting. In order to change results, you must change behaviors. Behaviors drive results. For example, if you are unhappy with your weight, you will need to eat less, eat differently, and/or exercise more. You will have to change your behavior to lose weight. If you want to increase your sales, you will have to make more calls, develop a different sales technique, network better, and so on. You will have to change your behavior to increase your sales effectiveness. If you are in college and want to improve your grades, you will have to study more, study differently, get a mentor, take different types of courses, and so on. You will have to change your behavior to get better grades.

The interesting thing about behavior change is that outside motivations can cause you to temporarily change your behavior, but you cannot sustain behavior change unless you believe at the gut level that it is the right thing to do. You must change the subconscious premises that are driving the behavior. Individuals lose weight and then gain it back. Behavior change is ultimately driven by your beliefs. Beliefs drive behaviors, which drive results.

Coaching is about helping your team members (and you) understand the behaviors that produce superior results and helping them (you) understand (develop beliefs) that support the behavior. The belief must reinforce the concept that the behavior "makes the world a better place to live" and the behavior is in their (your) rational self-interest. Managing results is impossible. Coaching beliefs and behaviors that produce superior results is fundamental to successful leadership. Kelly King, my successor at BB&T, is primarily responsible for developing the beliefs and behaviors coaching model that we are discussing (although any misconceptions are my responsibility).

In this model, coaching is a critically important component. Coaching is about endlessly reenforcing the beliefs and behavior that produce the desired results. It is about constant feedback that rewards appropriate beliefs and behaviors and provides negative feedback for inappropriate beliefs and behaviors.

Instead of thinking of yourself as a leader or a manager, it may be more productive to view yourself as a coach or a teacher. Who wants to be managed? Not me. Most people, however, are open to being coached or taught. Coaching or teaching implies that someone is helping us achieve a higher level of performance. That effectively increases the control we have over our lives, which is a positive outcome.

Viewing yourself as a coach, especially early in your career, is a very helpful psychological mindset. It focuses you on the team members instead of on the results. Coaching/teaching yourself (self-taught) is a particularly effective way to achieve desired outcomes. Of course, the best leaders are by definition coaches/teachers. They are constantly coaching/teaching.

While I put a lot of attention on BB&T's investment in education, significant improvement in individual performance is based on thoughtful feedback from mentors and coaches or from self-coaching within the context of fundamental principles. This type of feedback occurs almost daily.

A critical component of coaching is what you believe and how you behave. Your team members have a deep understanding of your beliefs and behaviors. They observe your actions at a deeper level than your words. They have a fairly insightful comprehension of who you are. You lead by example, whether you like it or not. Of course, at some subconscious level you know who you are. Pretending you are someone else is self-destructive and organizationally destructive.

So be who you are, and if you do not like some aspect of who you are, change that aspect. Start by reflecting on the desired results. Maybe you get angry too easily or you fail to express your true opinions. After you define what different results you want, reflect on the behaviors that would be appropriate to produce this different outcome. Maybe you should always count to 10 before expressing an opinion in a potentially anger-creating situation. Maybe you should commit to always expressing your opinion if only to express agreement or disagreement. Then think—and this is difficult—about why you have been behaving in a manner that produces unsatisfactory results. What destructive belief do you hold that is causing the negative behavior, which produces a destructive result? What belief do you need to hold to reinforce the behavior you want to exhibit to produce the result you desire?

An example of this type of desirable behavioral change occurred when BB&T acquired a company and some individuals were being asked to move into roles that had a sales component. Initially they believed that selling was a negative from a customer perspective. To begin the process of change, we disconnected the behavior from the result and simply focused on behavior. We would ask the individuals moving into the sales role to just call their clients and honestly thank them for their business and then ask them if there was anything we could do for them. There were no expectations of sales, but paying attention to one's clients often increases sales, especially in the long term. In this process it is important not to measure results just yet. Change the behavior and the results will change. Of course, if you honestly thank your clients for their business and they understand that you would honestly like to help them, they will give positive feedback when this happens. The salespeople can then grasp the appropriate win-win relationship, and selling and service become one. They have changed their belief.

In fund-raising, I have observed individuals who do an excellent job describing to potential sponsors why they should contribute to an organization but fail to ask for the donation. They believe the sponsors will be offended if they ask for funding. In fact, the sponsors expect to be asked and wonder why you have wasted their time if you do not ask. Clearly, this is a case where the fund-raiser needs to be incentivized to ask and will find over time that the potential sponsors' positive reaction to being asked (even if they do not make the contribution) changes the development individual's beliefs.

If you would like to reduce your body fat, start exercising 45 minutes every day and/or decide to eat red meat only once a week and/or eliminate carbs, and so on. Focus on the behavior and the result will follow.

I believe that within the confines of the law of reality you can improve results in practically any part of your life. But you will have to work at it. Improvement is practically never free. Pick objectives that are important to you, whether personal or for your team. There are no free lunches.

Are there implications for leadership at the societal level? If you were president of the United States and job creation was below par and economic growth substantially below potential, what would you do? You might begin by asking who creates jobs and drives economic growth. The answer appears to be business leaders and entrepreneurs. What different behaviors would business leaders have to exhibit to produce future job growth and drive economic expansion? They would have to invest more. What would cause them to invest more? More government regulations? Probably not. More taxes? Certainly not. Being called "greedy"? Highly unlikely. More uncertainty? Not likely.

What behaviors should I exhibit as president to encourage business leaders to invest and create economic growth and meaningful jobs? Do you think recent presidential leadership has encouraged or discouraged business leaders to invest for the future? Leadership matters.

18

Continuous Improvement

Everything can be done better. There is always an opportunity for continuous improvement. This was a mindset at BB&T, which was reflected in performance evaluations and our Total Quality Management process. I am working hard to create this mindset at the Cato Institute. Unfortunately, some individuals view the suggestion that something can be done better as criticism. It is not necessarily criticism. Everything can be done better.

Organizations tend to concentrate power centrally. There is often some logic in this concentration, because the best intellectual talent and knowledge may be in the central group. However, most organizations are pyramids from a power perspective. Also, the home office tends to pull talent into support roles at the expense of client contact positions. One negative consequence is that information can be lost to the home office decision makers. Also, even if they have come from client contact roles, individuals often quickly develop a bias centered toward the home office.

An expression of this bureaucratic failing is overreaction to errors. If two of the client contact producers make serious mistakes, instead of treating the experience as a special cause, home office leaders decide the system has failed and needs more home office control. This reduces the risk of error for the home office department, but it often makes the whole organization less responsive to client needs and more bureaucratic.

To know where you should change and to understand when your changes are truly improvements, feedback is required. Previously we discussed feedback from clients, which is critical, but employee feedback is also essential. Unhappy employees will create service problems.

BB&T used employee surveys, but our most productive tool was from meeting with employees systematically and listening carefully to their concerns. When I was CEO, BB&T operated with 33 community banks. I would visit each of these banks in a systematic fashion. Some members of our executive management team would visit with me, regardless of their responsibilities, so that all the members of executive management visited a number of community banks each year. We would begin with a breakfast with 30 or so of our highest-performing frontline employees such as tellers and customer service representatives. There would be four round tables, with one person from executive management or the regional leadership team and 7 to 8 frontline employees at each table. It is amazing how much you can learn by asking questions and soliciting feedback from the people who impact your clients every day.

The feedback from a single employee may not be that meaningful. However, if you hear a recurring theme from a number of high-performing customer contact employees, there must be an issue that requires action. It was also interesting how many times our best client contact employees would clearly define a problem that was creating service quality problems for our clients and the home office departments, managed by strong leaders, would adamantly claim the problem was not a problem. As CEO you would think that because someone asked for a problem to be fixed, action would be taken. Unfortunately, since people at the home office department would not admit there was a problem, they would not act to fix it. They usually were not direct about not acting, but for all intents and purposes, they did not act.

It is my strong belief that if your best frontline people, those who directly impact your clients, think there is a problem, there is a problem. But it is not just the home office staff who are filters; everyone in the chain of command can be a filter. On numerous occasions right before the breakfast, I would ask a regional management person if she considered issue x to be a problem in her region, and she would say no. However, the tellers a short time later, without any prodding, would bring up the issue. Few managers want to admit there is a problem when they already have the authority to at least partially fix the problem and have chosen not to do so. Again, if your best frontline people believe there is a problem, there is a problem. The leader needs to act, at a minimum to change the belief, and hopefully cure the actual problem.

After breakfast, we would have a meeting with our community bank leadership team when they could tell their story and provide feedback or ask questions of executive management. This meeting was followed by a luncheon with our management-level employees and advisory board members in the community bank. The luncheon was always a great learning experience because of the questions and feedback from the community leaders who served on these boards. It was easy to understand why they were successful. At the end of the luncheon, I made an overview presentation on BB&T followed by more Q&A. After lunch, we toured a number of branch offices and perhaps looked at potential locations for expansion.

We also toured our home office functions with a similar process. In the city with our primary operations functions, we would shake hands with as many as 2,000 people in a day. In the course of a year, I would shake hands with approximately 15,000 of our 31,000 employees and several thousand of our local advisory board members.

Banking is a personal business in which relationships matter. Even though we used a lot of videos for information purposes, there is nothing like seeing someone in person.

Many leaders fail because they do not receive meaningful feedback. Sometimes this is a personality issue in that they intimidate their team members, who are therefore hesitant to express the truth. Sometimes leaders only seek feedback from those who are most likely to agree with them. Many times there will be individuals who filter information from their perspective and for their purposes, so that the data that reaches the leader has been modified so much as to be misleading.

It is essential to create an environment wherein honest feedback is encouraged and in which there are processes that drive this feedback from the people who ultimately produce the product or serve the customer. That will enable the leader and the organization to learn. Many destructive decisions are made because leaders will not listen to or do not receive feedback that would radically change the decision.

Organizations that tolerate reasonable mistakes are better able to create effective feedback and are far more likely to learn more rapidly. A reasonable mistake is an error made that is consistent with the organization's mission and values and was an honest effort to improve outcome, even though the actual outcome was negative. Such organizations tend to be run by entrepreneurs and to have the ability to more effectively deal with change.

Creating effective feedback is cultural and systematic. Culturally, honest feedback should be encouraged and rewarded. Systematically, managers should be forced by the process to listen to the people who actually have to get the job done, as was done by BB&T with community bank visits.

There are some significant societal leadership implications of this issue. You would not want to vote for a president who was not able to get feedback from those who disagree with him. Consider: Is feedback likely to be more effective at the local level or at the national? Clearly, the closer to the customer (in the case of a government, its citizens) decisions can be made, the more likely the decision will reflect feedback from those who are affected by the decision. The Founding Fathers of the United States grasped this idea by trying to force as much authority as practical to the states and the citizens instead of to central control. How effective are federal government bureaucracies likely to be in receiving and acting on feedback? In this case, there is both a cultural and a system design issue.

I suspect most individuals reading this book realize that centralized government bureaucracies are extraordinarily unlikely to receive or act on feedback even when the feedback would help the governmental department achieve its goals. Most voters probably realize this is true, and yet they often vote for more government despite the obvious dysfunctional results.

19

Creating Win-Win Partnerships: Mergers and Acquisitions

Viewing life in partnership terms is a generally healthy perspective. Successful friendships, teams, marriages, civic organizations, and local communities all have partnership characteristics. The key to successful partnerships is focusing on making the relationship win-win. Obviously, sometimes creating win-win relationships is almost impossible. To the degree practical, win-lose or lose-win partnerships should be avoided because they are likely to fail.

During my tenure at BB&T, we executed over 100 mergers. We approached mergers as creating win-win partnerships, which is one reason practically all of our mergers were successful. It was our responsibility to analyze the facts thoroughly and objectively to be sure that a merger was in our constituents', specifically our shareholders', best interest. Secondly, we thoroughly analyzed why it was rational to believe a partnership with BB&T would be beneficial to the majority of the constituents of our potential merger partner.

Let me describe the merger process at BB&T. While this is a concrete example, hopefully you will see the general principle applicable to practically all cases of creating partnerships.

The first question to be asked is: Why are you interested in creating this partnership (or category of partnership)? In terms of bank acquisitions part of our motivation was that without the growth potential from mergers, we did not have the scale to be successful in a consolidating industry. We could have chosen to sell instead of grow. However, we were convinced that our culture and operating model were superior to that of the potential acquirers. Even though our shareholders would receive a premium on the front end, we would outearn the premium over time as an independent company. Also, given the characteristics of our shareholders, most would hold the acquirer's stock for the long term, and we were not willing to effectively sanction the potential acquirer's stock as a healthy long-term investment. This position turned out to be totally correct. Even shareholders who received significant front-end premiums but chose to hold the stock of Wachovia/First Union or Bank of America (who would have practically acquired BB&T) have been sorry.

In the case of nonbank acquisitions, our motivation was to diversify our income stream to reduce risk. Most of our bank acquisitions were plain-vanilla companies with limited sources of revenues except from lending. This concentration of income from lending made us more vulnerable to economic cycles.

The general principle is that we were clear about what our motivation was in pursuing these mergers. The mergers were not ends in themselves but goals toward creating a rapidly growing but relatively low-risk business, which is what we achieved. When doing a merger becomes an end in itself, the merger usually fails. The same goes for partnerships.

Before becoming involved in a merger, it is critical that your own organization be running well. You are extremely unlikely to fix a broken system with an acquisition. Our community bank structure allowed us to easily accommodate community banks and savings and loan (S&L) acquisitions.

The next step in bank/S&L acquisitions was to broadly define the type of institution we were interested in acquiring. We decided the potential partner had to meet several criteria. There needed to be a reasonable cultural fit, or we would not be able to effect the cultural integration, which is essential to a successful merger. (Are your partners reasonable cultural fits?) Secondly, in general, we did not want to "bet the bank," so we would focus on smaller or cleaner mergers, where if something went wrong it would not sink our ship. We wanted to build a franchise that would be competitive in the long term, so we put energy into in-market mergers in which we would have a relatively large market share, which created efficiencies and brand value.

It was also decided that our focus would be on solid or medium performing institutions. Dysfunctional organizations are typically difficult to fix. Also, it is hard to improve the performance of high performers. Why would a high performer sell if there were not hidden issues?

Of course, the economics had to work from our shareholders' perspective. We created rigorous criteria in terms of the impact on earnings per share, book value per share, and the rate of return. More important, discipline was applied to ensure we did not fool ourselves by being overly optimistic with projections of savings and revenues. In this regard, the board members were told that for 10 years after an acquisition was effected, they would be provided with a report on how well the acquisition performed relative to our projections. It is tough to remind your board for 10 years that you made a significant mistake, so this discipline encouraged rational, objective analysis.

Within this broad context, the next step was to develop a list of our top 100 prospects. The selection of prospects was based on cultural fit, economics of the acquisition, and the probability of the preferred acquisition choosing to sell. Solid institutions that might have a challenge maintaining their performance were prime candidates. Management succession was often a key issue from a potential seller's perspective. We also focused on community banks and thrifts that had been in business a long time. These institutions were more likely to have a loyal client base. We tended to avoid companies that we perceived were created to be sold because this type of business is usually a short-term profit maximizer, and maintaining profitability would be a challenge.

After defining our list of possible partners, we began a systematic calling process. Our calling effort was led by Burney Warren, a CEO from one of our early acquisitions, who knew the thrift and community bank industry. Before making a call, we would carefully analyze the potential partner, looking for areas where a merger with us would objectively be to their benefit. When meeting with them, it was critical to communicate that we understood their strengths and weaknesses and that our discussion was based on the concept of a win-win partnership. We absolutely did not want to talk people into joining our team if they were not clear about what it looked like to be part of BB&T and what the cost and benefits of the partnership would be.

A merger, like a marriage, should be entered into in the context of creating a successful long-term relationship. You do not want to outsmart or mislead in any way your future partner. If people there are not objectively energized by the potential of the partnership, then it will be better for both parties to pass on the potential relationship.

If people from the potential merger partner were interested in moving forward, then they were invited to our headquarters, where we told them the BB&T story and introduced our key executive managers. In telling the story, the financials were discussed; fortunately, BB&T's financial results were impressive. However, the focus was on culture. We believed that the merger partners who grasped the significance of culture to long-term economic performance would be the best partners for us.

When the potential partner was interested in discussing price, we shared our analysis of the economics of the merger from both our and their perspective and how we had arrived at the price we were willing to offer. One important area was to discuss potential cost savings. Some of our competitors in the acquisition business would justify paying higher prices by assuming very aggressive cost savings. We would point out that their cost savings looked as if the merger partner's employees would be losing their jobs. Also, we would ask what would happen to their business and their customers if such aggressive cost savings were implemented. Our experience indicated that an acquirer who paid too much for one company would pay too much for the next company and would be forced to cut costs too aggressively, which destroyed the business it had acquired. If the shareholders of the first acquirer held onto the stock of the acquiring company, which many community bank shareholders would do, partially for tax reasons, they would be worse off in the long term. For example, First Union was a very aggressive acquirer; the sellers ultimately were sorry in the long term.

In general, we were not interested in bid acquisitions in which price was the primary criterion because that type of mindset often represented a cultural difference between BB&T and the potential merger partner.

Our calling effort was very systematic because we were selling the culture and long-term performance of BB&T, not the maximum short-term gain. Burney and I would call on companies every quarter and let them know we were interested, following their performance, and keep them up-to-date on BB&T. In the case of one of our larger acquisitions, we called on three different CEOs over a period of almost 15 years before they chose to sell. However, when they chose to sell, they only talked to us.

The postacquisitions process is as important as the premerger strategy. Some mergers fail because they are intrinsically destructive deals. More mergers fail because of how the employees are treated after the merger is announced. It is critical to understand that the most valuable asset a company has is its employees. We systematically refined our process through a Total Quality Management procedure as we learned from each of our mergers.

On the date a merger was announced, we would hold an all-employee meeting in smaller companies and an all-manager meeting in larger businesses. Where it was not practical to have all employees attend, we would prepare a DVD for viewing by all employees the next morning.

At this meeting, the leaders of our merger partner would outline the reasons they had chosen to sell to BB&T. I would then discuss BB&T's strategy and culture with a primary focus on what it looked like to work for BB&T. We were very transparent to the employees about the benefits and the negatives of the merger from their perspective. Our goal was to eliminate as much ambiguity as possible. Ambiguity is more difficult to handle than bad news.

Our focus was primarily on how to make the merger work for the employees of the company we were acquiring within the context of the economics of the transaction. For example, when mutual thrifts (depositor-owned institutions) were acquired, we committed to keep all the employees of the thrift regardless of their job because these mergers were very beneficial to our shareholders.

In the typical community bank acquisition, we would commit to keep all the client contact employees even if the merger was in a market where there were overlapping branches with BB&T, some of which would be closed. We knew we might have extra staff when the merger was consummated, but normal turnover would take care of this problem. The positive morale of the client contact employees of the company being acquired would be transmitted to the client, and client retention and goodwill would more than offset the fact that it would take more time to realize the potential cost savings.

In the case of home office employees, it was not practical to guarantee everyone a job, as a number of functions would need to be centralized. Nevertheless, the goal was to provide as many opportunities as possible to potentially displaced employees. For example, we would offer positions to all satisfactorily performing home office employees who were willing to move. There was enough turnover in the total BB&T system to find positions for these mobile employees. Any home office employee who was willing to be trained to fill a client contact role would be given the opportunity to do so.

In a number of larger mergers we placed home office functions in the headquarters city of the company we were acquiring. For example, in the case of United Carolina Bank, we chose to locate our systemwide call center in the bank's headquarters city, Whiteville, North Carolina, even though this is a small town. When BB&T acquired One Valley Bank, we moved a number of home office style functions to Charleston, West Virginia. Even though on the surface these might not be cost-optimizing decisions, the morale benefits and the psychological impact in the markets were easily worth the cost. One interesting aspect is that the quality of employees in these locations was excellent and they were experienced bankers, so we were staffing functions better than if we were to hire marginal employees in BB&T's existing locations.

One humorous aside about the Whiteville location: when Bill Clinton was president, he wanted to encourage the expansion of the Internet to rural markets. He chose to visit Whiteville. However, because of our systemwide call center, Whiteville already had a world-class sophisticated technology hub. He did shake hands with our employees, and they loved it. He said their names, which impressed everyone. Of course, our employees wore name tags.

In addition to trying to find job opportunities at BB&T, we also had a first-class outplacement service for those employees who could not find a fit. Our goal was to find a job as good or better for the displaced employees than the one they had at the merger partner. We did not always have 100 percent success, but a large portion of displaced employees found comparable or better jobs.

BB&T offered a very generous severance package to any displaced employees. When BB&T acquired Colonial Bank, which was a transaction assisted by the Federal Deposit Insurance Corporation (FDIC), we were not required to pay any severance to displaced employees. However, we voluntarily chose to incur approximately $25 million in severance cost. The general principle is that the employees who stay will very closely observe how you treat the employees who leave. If you do not treat the displaced employees fairly, the employees who stay will assume you will not treat them fairly.

There are a couple of other aspects regarding how employees are treated that are critical to success. First, the primary reason employees fail in their new jobs is because they have not been trained properly. As indicated earlier, employee education is one of BB&T's hallmarks. In mergers we focused on training the employees from the merged companies so they could be successful in their new roles. When the conversion to BB&T's computer systems would take place, we would send experienced, high-performing BB&T employees to every new branch for a couple of weeks to deal with any issues with the system that the new employees might be unfamiliar with. The details are hard for individuals to remember when they move from training to the real world. These "buddy" relationships would often continue for years after the BB&T employees returned to their normal responsibilities.

Even though the Colonial acquisition was an FDIC bid deal and we did not know whether we would be successful or not, BB&T sent several hundred employees to the Colonial market the Thursday before the winning bid was announced. When we won the bid from the FDIC at 5 p.m. on Friday, a BB&T employee went to each Colonial branch to reassure the Colonial employees that we wanted them as part of the BB&T team. We expressed that we knew they were important and that their executive management may have made some bad decisions but that did not mean that the individuals in the branches were not excellent bankers.

We also tried to keep both employees and clients fully informed as we moved through the merger process. Because of bureaucratic red tape, it typically took six to nine months from announcement of a merger to consummation. This delay created much anxiety. I wish bureaucrats had to suffer the same unnecessary heartache. Anyway, we worked hard to keep everyone updated to reduce uncertainty.

In addition to a very rigorous process for employee integration, we had an extremely rigorous process for the system's conversions. A real disaster occurs if the clients' accounts are negatively impacted because of system mistakes. We had a "10,000"-step set of procedures to drive system conversion issues to zero. By the end of my career, system conversion errors were practically nonexistent.

We discovered a strategic opportunity early in the growth process. In the late 1980s, the S&L industry was in serious trouble. S&Ls had been making long-term, fixed-rate mortgages for many years and financing those mortgages with short-term savings deposits and certificates of deposit. When the Federal Reserve rapidly and radically raised interest rates in the early 1980s, many S&Ls failed because of the interest rate risk in their portfolios. Many of the surviving institutes began to invest in higher-risk commercial mortgages because they could earn variable interest rates, thereby reducing their interest rate risk. However, commercial real estate lending can be very risky from a credit risk perspective, especially if your institution does not have expertise in this area, which most S&Ls did not. In the late 1980s and early 1990s there was a second shakeout in the thrift industry. An economic correction driven by errors by the Federal Reserve and changes in tax policy, accelerated by excessive optimism in commercial real estate lending, led to major credit losses in the industry and many S&L failures.

Because of the visibility of many failures in the thrift industry, the negative publicity about the industry was deafening. This publicity significantly damaged the reputation of even well-managed, healthy S&Ls. At the time banks could not acquire S&Ls due to an archaic law that forced the separation of the banks and thrifts. However, it seemed to us to be inevitable that the law would be repealed, as additional capital would have to be attracted to the S&Ls. The best place for this capital to come from was banks. We announced the first acquisition in the country of a stock-owned thrift by a bank before the law even changed, and we were able to consummate the deal after banks were allowed to buy S&Ls.

BB&T carefully targeted the healthy thrifts, which were a subset of the industry. We focused on mergers in our current market area where we could increase market share and thereby improve efficiency. BB&T was the most successful S&L acquirer in the country. Before my tenure as CEO, we were somewhat late to the acquisition game, so the thrift acquisition program was essential to creating an efficient franchise on which to expand the rest of our business.

Many banks were unsuccessful in their thrift acquisitions and lost most of the customer relationships postacquisition. BB&T was the most successful acquirer because we purchased healthy companies and because we intensely focused on making the acquisition a success for the employees of the thrift. Many bankers viewed thrift employees as second class. Our experience was that the average thrift employee was equal to the average bank employee in terms of talents and abilities. However, they may not have been properly trained relative to bank-level products. We focused on training the thrift employees to make them successful.

One fun story relates to an early healthy thrift acquisition. Burney and I called on the CEO of a large, old-fashioned thrift that, despite the company's strength, was losing business due to the extremely negative publicity about the industry.

The CEO was an old, grizzled veteran. When we sat down in his office, the first thing he did was pull out a large pistol and place it on his desk pointing out how he had chased a robber out of the bank the week before. Subtle message.

We then discussed the potential benefits to all his constituents—clients, employees, board members, and community—from a merger with BB&T. Objectively, the benefits were very positive. However, after we were about halfway through our discussion, he stood up and sort of grabbed me by the collar and led us out of his office. Yet he must have seen the benefits because two weeks later he called, and we made a deal in a short time. Even though he really did not want to sell the company where he had worked for many years, upon reflection he realized that it was clearly in the best interest of the people he cared about to make an agreement with BB&T.

In addition to bank and thrift acquisitions, BB&T was extraordinarily successful in insurance brokerage mergers. At the time we started growing our insurance business, banks in general were prohibited from being in the industry due to antiquated regulations designed to protect insurance agents from bank competition.

BB&T was a state-chartered bank, and we were grandfathered because we had acquired an insurance agency in the 1920s as the result of a loan default. In the late 1980s we still had this small agency located in an eastern North Carolina farm town. Because the agency was so small, we planned to sell it, but before doing so decided to analyze the market situation. Our analysis indicated that the insurance agency business should be consolidated because the current structure was extremely inefficient. Also, potential insurance clients were willing to purchase insurance from a bank. Furthermore, because we had strong, publicly traded stock, we could potentially offer a better economic package to possible sellers. In addition, this fit with our overall strategy of increasing fee income, thereby diversifying our income stream.

Strategically, we decided to try to purchase the best agencies in growth markets in the BB&T banking footprint. An early acquisition was one of the most highly regarded and largest agencies in our market area. The leaders of this agency were well known for their opposition to banks being in the insurance business.

When we objectively outlined the benefits of the merger, however, they decided to sell to BB&T. This was a thunderbolt in the insurance brokerage business because of the high-quality reputation of the company and that agency's past opposition to banks being in the business.

Our executional strategy was to work hard and support with contracts the retention of the entire sales force. The owners typically were salespeople and they could keep their current sales roles, often with increased time for selling. They could take a private company public in a tax-free transaction, creating liquidity for their family, and capture substantial additional dividend income from BB&T stock ownership.

The cost savings for BB&T were in the backrooms of the agencies, which were typically not efficient and were often viewed as a hassle for the sales-dedicated owners. We offered better systems and worked hard to be fair to any displaced employees.

Also, as we continued to roll up agencies, the insurance companies whose products we sold took notice because they realized the traditional agency system was not efficient and that we had developed a better model. We began to be able to negotiate better deals with the insurance companies, which allowed us to be more competitive in driving revenue (and sales incentive for employees) for the acquired agencies.

Furthermore, some of the agencies we acquired had a specialty in a specific insurance product. We could cross-refer from the other agencies driving revenue growth.

Initially we had expected that it would be easy to cross-sell our banking clients basic insurance products. This turned out to be far more difficult to execute than expected. In fact, most banks that entered the insurance agency business failed because they focused too much on selling to banking clients and did not achieve scale to leverage the insurance companies.

One reason cross-selling was difficult is because bankers tended to refer the wrong clients to the insurance agencies. The banking clients that were the most willing to talk to the agency were the ones who had problems getting insurance (maybe they had a DWI on their driving record). Over time, BB&T has radically improved its cross-sell effectiveness, but there is a long learning curve for both bankers and agents. The key decision early on was to focus on having a world-class insurance agency system and then to drive cross-selling. If we truly were able to deliver better insurance products and services to our banking clients, then the cross-sell would naturally follow.

BB&T's initial acquisitions were local property and casualty insurance agencies. Subsequently, we made a critical strategic decision to acquire a large wholesale broker, which took our agency system to a higher plane. A wholesale broker helps local agencies place insurance that is difficult to underwrite, because the wholesale broker has developed relationships with specialty insurance carriers and can deliver enough volume to allow the carrier to diversify within a higher-risk portfolio. We also acquired a managing general underwriter (MGU). This is another specialty niche where the MGU has such skilled underwriters that big insurance companies like Berkshire Hathaway allow the MGU to underwrite the risk even though the insurance company assumes the risk.

BB&T recently acquired a large wholesale life insurance broker and now operates the second-largest property and casualty wholesale insurance broker and the largest life insurance wholesale insurance broker in the United States. The retail agencies feed business to the wholesale brokers, who also serve many other retail brokers. The combination has taken BB&T from a small town farm agency in 1989 to the sixth-largest insurance distributor in the world currently. The diversification of income created by the insurance agency business helped BB&T's performance during the recent financial crisis, as anticipated.

In addition, as a complementary business, BB&T has made acquisitions in the insurance premium finance business, becoming the second-largest insurance premium financer in the United States and the largest in Canada.

The real architect of this very successful and well-executed acquisition program is Wade Reece, a North Carolina "country boy." Here is a story about Wade that you may find interesting. We had unsuccessfully tried to hire leadership from the insurance broker industry to manage our agency acquisition program. After failing with outside hires, we decided to turn to a proven banking manager. When I visited with Wade without disclosing my long-term goals, I asked him what he thought of our insurance business. He said it "stunk" and did not have a future. After we convinced him that he would be given complete latitude to make necessary changes and would be totally supported by executive management, he later agreed to take over the agency system. About eight weeks after he started managing the system, I asked him what he thought. He said there was great potential and the agency system had a bright future—a very appropriate change in attitude and perspective.

The final acquisition area is noninsurance, nonbank acquisitions, again driven by an effort to diversify income. We made a conscious decision to do 10 small-venture capital acquisitions of financially related businesses including considering our clients who were in financially related businesses. Several of the acquisitions failed. Some were mediocre. Two turned into home runs.

One of the home runs is an interesting story. BB&T purchased a subprime automobile finance company at exactly the wrong time in the credit cycle. Prime-grade auto finance is one of BB&T's core businesses, and we thought there would be synergies between the prime and subprime businesses. The owner of the subprime business was very smart, and he saw the correction coming and sold at the peak. Be careful in buying a business from someone who knows a lot more about the industry than you do. The key to success in the industry is to be sure the borrower makes a substantial down payment, because default rates will inevitably be high. Also, a substantial interest rate must be charged, because there will be significant credit losses.

Because the subprime auto business had been making record profits, competition had intensified and down-payment requirements were reduced and interest rates cut. When the shakeout came, losses were far more than anticipated. By the way, the primary culprit in creating problems reflected in the automobile industry during the recent financial crisis was GMAC (now Ally), the one-time auto finance arm of General Motors, which has been bailed out twice by U.S. taxpayers. GMAC, in order to sell cars, started providing low-down-payment, low-interest-rate financing to subprime borrowers, ultimately driving high defaults, helping create a bubble in the auto markets, which crushed the auto industry. Of course, since GMAC (Ally) has been bailed out by the taxpayers, it will certainly make the same mistakes again—you can bet on it.

Anyway, for over 10 years, every time I made the report described earlier on the performance of our acquisitions to our board, it was necessary to describe this merger as a "disaster." There was legitimate pressure from the board and some members of executive management to sell the business. In fact, First Union (which became Wachovia) had purchased a significantly larger but similar business; it liquidated that business and lost 100 percent of its investment.

We stuck with the business, consistently improving our management and processes until we unquestionably became the best underwriter and most efficient competitor in the business. I believed that this was a good business long term because in our type of market our client base needed to be able to finance a car to get to work. Many Hispanic immigrants in particular had not established credit scores, and without a legitimate subprime auto lender they would not be able to purchase transportation.

Over time our irrational competitors failed one by one, and we grew our business. In recent years, this product line has made a very significant contribution to BB&T's financial performance. Is there a lesson in this story? There are certainly times to exit businesses. However, one of BB&T's core strengths is outstanding operations. Assuming your organization has financial staying power, if you are in an industry in which being a world-class operator can create competitive advantage and the product serves a legitimate need, running the business extremely well will produce satisfactory results, as irrational competitors will eventually exit. Let the other firm make the big mistakes. Do not let incompetent competitors incent you to do anything irrational.

I hope you can see a series of organizational leadership insights in these stories. Strategy matters, process matters, rational decision making matters, but it all must come together through the excellent integration of the human beings involved in the process. Doing your best to create a win-win environment for as many partners as possible leads to success.

Are there any societal implications for the merger activities just described? I think there is a general lesson. For partnerships to work, they must be based on voluntary agreements. You may say that the employees of the companies we acquired did not always volunteer to be acquired. True, but they had the option of leaving. The employees who stayed volunteered to stay.

Successful partnerships cannot be forced. And yet successful partnerships of all types are essential to human well-being. Government is all about force. Governments have police, armies, and jails to enforce their edicts. Therefore, in the long term government-forced partnerships will not work. Again, you may say there are government/private "partnerships" in which the partnership is voluntary. Maybe it is voluntary in terms of the stated partner; however, if taxpayer money is being used, then one of the "partners," the taxpayer, is not a voluntary participant. The failure rate in government/private partnerships is high, especially if the secondary consequences are properly considered.

Because successful partnerships must be based on voluntary exchange and the government is fundamentally about force, the government should limit its activity to preventing the initiation of force by private individuals if we want optimal outcomes in terms of economic growth.

CEOs tell stories. Hopefully, you will find the following stories interesting even though they are peripheral to our discussion.

In 1995, my company, BB&T, and another bank our size, Southern National, entered into a merger of equals (which turned into a very successful transaction, something that is unusual for mergers of equals). In any event, right after the merger was consummated, there was a special meeting of the North Carolina Bankers Association at Bank of America's (then NationsBank) headquarters in Charlotte, North Carolina. When I walked into the meeting, Hugh McColl, CEO of NationsBank, immediately greeted me with the comment, "Allison, you are lucky to be here. We had decided to take you guys out of your deal, and we were an inch from making an offer but got concerned you might find a way to sell to somebody else." I quickly went to the bathroom to catch my breath. A near-death experience. (Sorry, I did not see a bright light.)

A little background, NCNB/NationsBank/Bank of America (same organization with new names) and First Union/Wachovia (the same organization with different names) had both coveted BB&T. The only way I was able to keep either organization from making an unfriendly offer was to play them against each other. I told Hugh that he could make an offer that would probably force us to sell, but I thought I could direct the sale to First Union. I told Ed Crutchfield, who was CEO of First Union, that if he forced the issue, I thought I could direct the sale to Bank of America. Of course, in order to earn the right from a shareholders' perspective to remain independent, we had to outperform the potential acquirers, which we did.

This is a complete aside, but an interesting story. The weekend before Wachovia (which had been First Union) decided to purchase Golden West, Ken Thompson, Wachovia's CEO, had tried very hard to get me to come to Charlotte to participate in a golf tournament. I am fairly certain that he intended to put a hard press on for Wachovia to purchase BB&T. Bank of America was preoccupied at the time. I did a song and dance to avoid the golf tournament.

Golden West was the leading proponent of the "pick a payment" mortgage. The Golden West acquisition contributed significantly to Wachovia's subsequent failure and sale to Wells Fargo. Since BB&T went through the financial crisis without a single quarterly loss, if Wachovia had bought BB&T instead of Golden West, the financial industry would look very different today. Oh well.

Becoming CEO and Making a Lot of Money: Self-Development

I AM OFTEN ASKED BY STUDENTS WHETHER MY INTENTION WHEN I joined BB&T was to become CEO and make a lot of money. I liked being CEO and enjoyed earning a lot of money, but neither of those things was an objective. My goal was always to do whatever I did better than it ever had been done before and to understand how what I did related to the rest of the organization.

In this context, self-development has been a personal obsession. Hopefully, my example might provide some general principles, especially for younger readers. My focus has been in three broad areas: (1) technical knowledge/skills (for example, economics, business, and banking), (2) philosophy, and (3) psychology (especially self-awareness).

In pursuit of a knowledge of economics, I took extra economics courses in undergraduate school even though I was a business major. I took additional economics courses in my MBA program. Most of this material was of limited value except to give me an understanding of the vocabulary on the neo-Keynesian school that is still very prevalent.

Frankly, most of the economic theory in the leading textbooks of the 1960s and 1970s is misleading. In my opinion, the fact that most of the CEOs of major financial institutions and the Federal Reserve bureaucrats were educated on neo-Keynesian economic theory in college contributed to the financial crisis.

I also read and reread John Maynard Keynes's famous book *The General Theory of Employment, Interest, and Money*. It is scary to me that Keynes is taken seriously based on this book. It is a total rationalization for big government. You should read it along with *Das Capital* by Karl Marx. That these "thinkers" are still having a material influence on public policy decisions should be of great concern to you.

I learned economics largely out of the classroom by reading practically everything written by Ludwig von Mises (including *The Theory of Money and Credit* and *Human Action*), Friedrich Hayek, and Milton Friedman. I asked all members of the BB&T executive management to read both *The Theory of Money and Credit* and *Human Action* and gave copies to our board members. If all CEOs of banks and all members of the Federal Reserve Board had been required to read *The Theory of Money and Credit*, the recent financial crisis could have been avoided. Unfortunately, Alan Greenspan, then head of the Federal Reserve, also certainly read both books and ignored their lessons. *Economics in One Lesson* by Henry Hazlitt and *The Road to Serfdom* by Friedrich Hayek are very worthwhile reading.

Most of my business technical education was from undergraduate and graduate business school courses. After graduation, I focused on biographies of successful business leaders. In accounting, I had taken a number of accounting courses in undergraduate and graduate business schools, but after beginning work I read all the textbooks that one would cover in obtaining a master's degree in accounting. Accounting is the language of business and must be thoroughly understood to make financial decisions. Accounting and economics are only superficially aligned. One must be able to understand how to intellectually convert accounting language into real economic calculations. I read numerous textbooks and general books on banking and attended a master's degree program at the Stonier Graduate

School of Banking. I wrote a thesis for my master's degree in business and one for the banking graduate program, both of which were used to improve decision making at BB&T.

I developed a somewhat unique "hobby" for a businessperson—the study of philosophy. While my study of philosophy was driven by a personal desire to understand fundamental principles, it has had a significant impact on any success I have achieved in business. Here are a few thoughts about studying philosophy. In my opinion, most modern philosophy (not all) is academic jargon that is disconnected from reality.

You probably want to read Plato, even though his metaphysics is irrational. According to Plato, what we know is really shadows on the cave wall reflecting the real reality, which is knowable only to philosopher kings. It is amazing that this detached-from-reality idea, in all kinds of variations, is prevalent in much philosophy to this day. Immanuel Kant is considered one of the three greatest philosophers (with Plato and Aristotle). Good luck reading Kant.

The philosophers that influenced me the most are Aristotle, Thomas Aquinas, John Locke, and Ayn Rand. In the case of Plato, Aristotle, and Aquinas, I recommend you read interpretations of their writings such as John Randall's *Philosophy: An Introduction* before you attempt to read the originals. Locke is relatively easy to read from the original. Of course, Rand is the most accessible, because she primarily put her philosophy in novels, including *Atlas Shrugged* and *The Fountainhead*. Leonard Peikoff's *Objectivism: The Philosophy of Ayn Rand* is an extraordinarily powerful book. Anyone who is familiar with Rand will see her ideas reflected in my own philosophy that I've shared throughout this book. She has had a huge impact on my thinking. If you have not read *Atlas Shrugged*, you should begin immediately. It is extraordinarily relevant to today's cultural environment and, although a novel, is the best book ever written on political economy.

In any event, studying philosophy will improve your critical thinking ability and help you understand the arguments for and against many fundamental ideas that you take for granted. You have a philosophy, whether you like it or not.

One of the most beneficial learning experiences for me has been my efforts to become more self-aware and in the process to gain a different understanding of the psychological motivations of others. As discussed previously, in the early 1990s BB&T purchased a psychological development company, Farr Associates, whose primary focus is self-awareness. Through participating in numerous workshops and other programs taught by this company, I have developed a far deeper understanding of my subconscious psychological drives and their impact on my behavior. Also, I have a much better understanding of what motivates others and how to read their behavior. Of course, this does not mean I have achieved "guru" status, but I am less crazy and happier than I would have been without this process.

Many otherwise intelligent individuals make very destructive decisions based on irrational subconscious psychological premises. They believe they are acting rationally when their actions are irrational. However, these irrational actions flow logically from the irrational psychological premises they hold. Companies spend far too little on helping their employees, especially key decision makers, become aware of their subconscious psychological drivers.

Unfortunately, much of what passes as psychology in the corporate world consists of bromides, clichés, and political correctness. This has given psychological development a bad reputation.

Much of the current focus on psychological development is on strengthening your strengths. There certainly can be benefits from this process. But the real power is in confronting your demons— your deepest weaknesses. The problem with confronting your demons is that doing so is not much fun. Also, a few individuals may react so fearfully as to make the process negative. Nevertheless, for most people, these negative beliefs are below the surface and yet they know they are there. When they surface and are confronted, much of their power goes away.

Much of my personal development was based on actual experience, including making many mistakes. Some advice I am giving employees at the Cato Institute who are relatively early in their careers is to use every day as a learning experience just as one would learn in an academic environment. Refuse to evade; stay in focus. Work to develop concepts that help you make decisions from the concrete life experiences of every day.

I tried to encourage lifelong learning by example for our leadership group. To this day, I read at least one serious book each month.

At BB&T, I would send the best of the books to our leadership team. My primary Christmas presents to our board members were books. I also took two weeks a year for education: one week devoted to job-specific education and one week to philosophy.

One more thought about money. It is nice to have money. It provides a sense of both security and flexibility. However, after a base level of compensation, maybe $100,000 per year in today's dollars, the value of having money falls significantly. Nevertheless, earning money is tremendously rewarding, even if you give it all away. Earning money in a free society is a symbol of productivity and has a meaningful psychological reward. It is the earning, not the having, that is valuable.

That's enough about my education to become a successful CEO. Here are the general concepts that follow: get clear about your fundamental beliefs (philosophy and values), become self-aware and own your emotions (psychological), understand the theory and practice of your chosen field (technical expertise), and be a lifelong experiential learner. Go for it.

21

Effective Leadership
Is Integration

INTEGRATION, ACCORDING TO THE *OXFORD ENGLISH DICTIONARY*, IS "THE making up or composition of a whole by adding together or combining the separate parts or elements." Integration is the fundamental mental activity of effective leaders.

Reflect on the leadership process we have been discussing: (1) a vision that paints a picture of a better world; (2) a purpose/mission that defines the vision in more concrete terms in words and concepts; (3) strategies that are essential to the accomplishment of the purpose; (4) coaching that ensures the people involved in the process can effectively execute the strategies; and (5) values that set the fundamental principles under which the individuals on the team will operate.

The key to success is for each of the elements to be consistent with the others. All elements must be integrated to create a whole. It is the leader's ability to see the connections that bind together the whole that makes for effective, powerful, meaningful leadership.

Integration typically takes place in the subconscious, so oftentimes leaders do not know when the integration has occurred. It can be a series of subconscious ahas that lead to a whole. Because integrations often occur in the subconscious, it is sometimes difficult to explain to others why the integration is correct. However, understanding and proving the integration at the conscious level is necessary for effective communications and actions.

Sometimes leaders make subconscious integrations and then act on those integrations without bringing the thought process to consciousness. Loyal supporters may follow this type of leader, and the results can be successful. However, the results are unlikely to be optimal because the process of bringing the integration to consciousness almost always clarifies the action steps to accomplishment in the mind of the leader. Also, if the action plan is dependent on other people, the better they understand the why, the more likely they will be able to act in a manner consistent with the objective.

Certainly, there are successful leaders who can only integrate a subset of all the components of leadership outlined previously. The clearest example is strategic visionaries, described in Chapter 2, who can make an integration of trends in the economy or technology but cannot integrate on values or psychologically, and yet their organization produces outstanding results in economic terms. Of course, some leaders just get lucky.

In terms of human flourishing the best leaders integrate across all the components of leadership. Their organizations/departments/groups will be successful in economic terms within the context of the rationally achievable outcomes. Equally important, the members of the team will have the opportunity to achieve meaningful work, again within the context of the rationally achievable outcome. Remember, human flourishing—happiness—is the end of the game.

Clearly, in leading yourself you want to have an integrated view of your life: vision, purpose, strategies, and values, all consistent and reinforcing. These concepts as applied to yourself must be consistent with reality, because Mother Nature, to be mastered, must be obeyed.

The integrations do not have to be at some profound deep level, nor do they have to be complex. They do need to be consistent with your abilities, and they must continue throughout your life as you systematically correct errors. The standard is not genius, nor is it acceptable to integrate at a level beneath your abilities.

Remember our discussion of concept formation in Chapter 4. Integration is a meta concept. It is seeing as much of the mosaic of Mother Nature and human nature as your mind is capable of putting together as a whole. It is critical to realize that you are the only one who can achieve integration for yourself. Obviously, there is an incredible amount to learn from others, including geniuses like Aristotle, whom we will never match in the ability to integrate. However, even when you are learning from others, the integration must be yours. Otherwise, if you blindly accept someone else's integrations, you will become dogmatic, which always leads to evasion and ultimately destroys an active mind.

Knowing that your goal is to integrate improves the probability that you will integrate effectively, just as knowing you are trying to form concepts to make decisions improves your ability to arrive at meaningful concepts. In a certain sense, integration is the ability to bring together your concepts so that they create a whole for living your life or leading your team.

You cannot avoid the task of self-leadership based on integration, but this is a far less complex task (albeit complex enough) than integration, where other human minds are involved. Each additional member of a team rapidly increases the complexity of the task. You may not be able to integrate effectively when other humans are involved or where you do not have control, just as I cannot integrate in the field of music. If this is the case, you may not want to strive to be in a leadership position.

There are individuals who have incredible capacity to integrate technical or mechanical factors far beyond my ability but who cannot integrate effectively when multiple human relationships are necessary to the completion of the task. Because management is often viewed as a higher level in organizations, sometimes these individuals are promoted to positions where they fail or are unhappy. Be cognizant of where you have the ability to integrate effectively, and search for work that fits your ability.

The fact that individuals are either born with and/or develop an ability to integrate in some intellectual spheres and not in others partially explains dysfunctional behavior in seemingly highly intellectual people—the absent-minded professor being a classic example.

I have wondered over the years why some geniuses have difficulty with human relationships. Steve Jobs, for one, was notoriously difficult to work with. My speculation is that these types of geniuses make integrations that the rest of us cannot grasp. The integrations are so clear and obvious to them that they assume we can make the same integrations. When we don't, they assume we are lazy, dishonest, argumentative, and/or dumb.

On a different plane, we can do the same thing to our children. We can get mad at them when they cannot see what we see. We sometimes accuse them of not listening when they actually do not understand. Also, because we have not brought the integrations from which we are acting to consciousness, we cannot really explain why the action suggested is appropriate, and we get angry (at ourselves, really) and take it out on our child.

This behavior sometimes happens with leaders. Leaders occasionally make integrations not obvious to a team member and, for the same set of reasons mentioned previously, express anger at the team member. This can be a particularly destructive behavior when a substantial number of the members of the team do not grasp the integration.

At the individual level, we sometimes make subconscious integrations inconsistent with our consciously held beliefs, and we may not want to let go of those consciously held beliefs. This can lead to frustrations, and anger (self-anger can become depression).

At the societal level, integration is even more critical for effective leadership. The vision, purpose, strategy, and values must be integrated, or social dysfunction will result. The ability of potential leaders to integrate is a critical issue in choosing whom to vote for along with that person's vision for our country. Lack of leadership experience is a critical limitation to someone who is going to have to integrate at the extraordinarily complex societal level.

Integration is the essential mental activity of effective leaders, especially in the context of human flourishing. Holding integration as a conscious goal will enable you to integrate better. Practicing integration will improve your ability to integrate. These are probably some innate drivers of our abilities to integrate. Try to find the areas where you are a successful integrator and where the integration gives you pleasure as an indication of the type of activity where you are most likely to achieve success and happiness.

22

Statism Versus Life, Liberty, and the Pursuit of Happiness

WE ARE ENGAGED IN A DEEP PHILOSOPHICAL BATTLE FOR THE future of Western civilization. The outcome of this battle will have a profound impact on the quality of human flourishing for many years. It is incorrect to see humankind as constantly progressing. In reality, human progress tends to be achieved in cycles. There is evidence that the Egyptian civilization regressed for thousands of years, and then progressed. From AD 400 until AD 1300, Western civilization regressed. Constant progress is not guaranteed. Ideas matter.

We will discuss the two relative extremes in the philosophical battle for the future of humankind. (There are more extreme positions, but these positions are not factors today.) Most individuals' beliefs fall between these more extreme positions. It is important to remember that in any compromise between good and evil, evil wins by definition. In any compromise between good food and poison, poison wins. Therefore, it is critical to decide which vision of the future you share and be sure that any public policies you support are moving in the direction you think is the best for you, your children, and your grandchildren.

On one side are the statists of all stripes. On the other side are the advocates of strictly limited government. This limited government position is best exemplified by classical liberalism/libertarianism, which will be discussed after we examine statism.

Statism is best typified by the modern progressive movement. Progressives can be viewed as radical liberals. They are supportive of more radical left ideas than most liberals. However, many liberals hold the same basic premises. There are many people who consider themselves conservatives who are statist at heart. They view the concrete role of the state as different from progressives, especially as it relates to civil liberties, but they are advocates of a powerful role for the state.

For example, one of the most visible leaders of the conservative/ Tea Party movement has declared that if the state does not make gay marriage and marijuana consumption illegal, the state is sanctioning these activities. By the same logic, if the state does not make excessive fat consumption illegal, the state is sanctioning obesity. Many more people die from obesity-related diseases than from marijuana consumption. Surely, the Big Mac should be illegal, based on this conservative/Tea Party leader world view. Of course, that leader would not support making Big Macs illegal, but failing to see the logical extension of his argument is a serious intellectual error.

Let's outline the premises that underlie the progressive world view and that of some of the more fundamental conservatives. One of their strongest premises, their most basic beliefs, is that humans are innately flawed because we are selfish. Notice: this is a strong belief on both the left and the right. To their credit, many on the religious right believe that an individual's relationship with the church and/ or directly with God is the best avenue to cure this natural deficiency. However, in certain avenues, such as gay marriage, gambling, and drug consumption, the state needs to step in and take over the church's place. The premise that human beings are innately flawed is why the state typically expands under so-called conservative governments, just slower than under liberal regimes.

The progressives do not trust the church or any private method to deal with this deadly human flaw. Their answer is unequivocally that the power (force) of the state is necessary. Communists (and Nazis) believed that human nature could be modified through education and indoctrination to serve the common good instead of individual self-interest. This indoctrination program did not work very well for either the Nazis or the communists. Modern progressives/liberals seem to recognize that modifying human nature is at minimum a difficult task. They believe in nudges, backed by a "gun," to incent the behavior they believe is in the common good, as they see it. Of course, as noted, "common good" is an oxymoron. Practically every action is positive for some people and negative for others.

The progressives are the modern-day supporters of Plato's philosopher king. They do not literally want a king. They believe an elite group of techno-bureaucrats—all of whom attended elite Ivy League universities (or similar institutions), have advanced degrees from these universities, and share the same political beliefs—should be the new philosopher kings. In the last presidential election, according to the student political advocacy group Campus Reform, 96 percent of contributions by Ivy League professors to the presidential race went to Obama. This illustrates how diverse and objective the education experience is in Ivy League schools.

The animating moral principle of the progressives is their view of social justice, which is egalitarian. As previously discussed, egalitarianism is extraordinarily destructive in all its variations. Equality before the law is essential for free and productive societies. However, equal opportunity is an extraordinarily misleading idea. I was not born with the incredible hand-eye coordination of Tiger Woods. The only way to give us equal opportunity is to cut off his right arm. The concept of equal outcome is equally destructive. The only way to create equal outcomes is to use force to take what someone has produced and give it to someone who has not earned it. Furthermore, since you cannot make the average people great, to create equality you have to make the great average. It gets worse, because in every sphere, by definition, one-half the population is below average; the common denominator for an egalitarian world is below average. While most progressives would not go to this extreme, this is the only logical conclusion of their argument for egalitarianism. Any other end point is totally arbitrary. Arguments tend to move to their logical conclusion until they become so obviously destructive there is a social push-back. The push-back is usually some form of tyranny, such as Vladimir Putin in Russia.

Also, while progressives would not drive the argument to its logical conclusion, they would far rather we be more equal even if we are all poorer. Even if unequal outcomes raise the standard of living and the quality of life for everyone, they believe these unequal outcomes are immoral in and of themselves.

Progressives and statists on the right are altruist collectivists. They believe that being selfish (acting in one's rational self-interest) is bad. Altruism is by definition "otherism." Everyone else is important but you. This concept leads directly to collectivism, wherein the collective instead of the individual is the measure of the good. Collectivism has morphed into groupism for many progressives and liberals. People are ascribed to the group they belong to—their race, sex, nationality, sexual preference, class, age, and so forth. Your membership in these groups basically determines who you are, including your political beliefs.

Of course, some groups are victims and other groups are oppressors. Progressives need victims to save. Being altruists, if there were no victims, they would not have a purpose. Nothing galls the progressives and liberals more than when a member of an oppressed group does not sing the politically correct song. Witness the Senate election of Clarence Thomas, an African American conservative, to the U.S. Supreme Court. Observe the Middle East, where Jews were originally viewed as the oppressed and were supported by the left. Now that Israel is successful, many on the left consider Israel to be the oppressor and the Palestinians the oppressed. Apparently, being successful makes you an oppressor. The only way to be successful and not be an oppressor is to give very generously to progressive causes. Of course, this may make you appear to be a hypocrite, such as Al Gore fighting climate change while flying around in his own business jet or Warren Buffett fighting the Keystone Pipeline while owning the BNSF (Burlington Northern Santa Fe) Railway, which benefits enormously from the lack of pipeline competition.

Based on these premises, progressives believe that government action based on the insights of elitists is both necessary and appropriate to cure practically all societal problems. Progressives believe individuals have a few limited rights. You have the right to free speech if you do not use your money to support a conservative candidate. You have the right to free speech as long as nothing you say could possibly be interpreted as offensive to any underprivileged group (which includes practically everyone except successful white males). Of course, if you run a business, you give up your right to free speech because your comments might be impacted by your selfish desire to make money.

Because of the overtly obvious failure of socialism throughout history, progressives tend to believe there is a role for markets, but not free markets. Through regulations they want the state to control economic activity, but executed through superficially private businesses. When something goes wrong, then the business, not the government, is blamed.

Some current examples of this process are how retail gun stores and for-profit colleges are being treated. The banking regulators are putting pressure on banks to terminate the banking services of both retail gun shops and for-profit colleges. The attack on retail gun stores is a deliberate effort to circumvent the Second Amendment by a progressive administration. The Obama administration has a very deep dislike for colleges that operate for profit, because profit is a destructive incentive in their world view; hence, the subtle attack on banking services provided to for-profit colleges.

For progressives good intentions are critical and the end justifies the means. The intention to advance the so-called common good is critical even if the outcome is not positive for the group that is supposed to be the beneficiary of the action. Individuals are unimportant relative to the good of the state, class, or whatever.

The classical liberal/libertarian view is almost the exact opposite of that of the progressives. Classical liberals/libertarians are individualists. They believe in the sanctity of the individual. They recognize that people act in their self-interest. However, they view this fact as a positive motivating force for economic success. They also believe individuals can and often are benevolent, including willing to support many charitable causes. Human beings are capable of doing many vile things. But they are also capable of greatness. The vile acts are practically always based on the use of force (and/or fraud); hence, the need for government to prevent the initiation of force.

In this context, classical liberals/libertarians see the role of government as protector of individual rights—to keep you from taking by force or fraud what I have earned and to keep me from taking by force or fraud what you have earned. Government should stay out of your pocketbook, and (in contrast to the position taken by many conservatives) it should stay out of your bedroom.

Although classical liberals/libertarians believe the role of government is very important in preventing and/or punishing the initiation of force, they also believe the role of government ought to be very limited. It is appropriate to have a military to defend the United States from foreign nations that would threaten or destroy individual rights. (But participation in the military must be voluntary—there should be no draft.) A police force is necessary to protect citizens from violence by local villains. A court system is necessary so everybody can settle legitimate disagreements without resorting to violence.

In a classical liberal/libertarian world, the government has the exclusive right to initiate force, but only in the defense of an individual's inherent rights. Individuals have the right to self-defense (the right to keep and bear arms), but individuals do not have the right to initiate the use of force. This is an exclusive right given to government. The power of government comes from the consent of the governed. Individuals have natural rights. Rights do not come from government; individual rights precede government.

Because the right to initiate the use of force is so terribly powerful, government must be strictly limited or it will inevitably abuse the rights of individuals. In fact, the abuse of individual rights throughout history has largely been done by government. Governments have killed, maimed, and tortured millions more people than criminals and terrorists combined. Governments always claim to be operating in the common good of the group they serve as they slaughter innocent people. In the United States today, libertarians believe our criminal justice system violates the rights of as many individuals as criminals do. One reason is we believe if there is not a victim, there is not a crime. Voluntary acts among consenting adults are not crimes, even if they are considered immoral by some. The government should not be in the morality business, if you want freedom. Government is only in the protection of your rights business. Marijuana consumption and a long list of other so-called crimes lack victims and therefore are not really crimes. Murder, theft, and fraud are crimes because there are victims. The difference between the police and the criminals is a thin line.

The purpose of the military from a classical liberal/libertarian perspective is to protect and defend the country from a real and present danger. The United States should not be roaming all over the world starting wars to make the world safe for democracy, as neoconservatives believe, or to right all wrongs, as liberals believe.

In a classical liberal/libertarian world the U.S. court system would be significantly more efficient than it is today. Of course, there would be far fewer laws and dramatically fewer crimes. In addition, there would not be punitive damages that make attorneys rich, and to eliminate frivolous lawsuits "loser pays" would almost certainly be the rule in courts of law. The regulatory state and the welfare state would not exist.

Let's look at the classical liberal/libertarian leadership model. The vision is a free and prosperous society based on the principles of individual liberty, free markets, limited government, and peace. The purpose is to create a world in which each individual is free to pursue her rational self-interest as a free and independent person as long as she does not violate the rights of others.

Strategically, the U.S. military would be limited and focused but able to defend the United States, but it would not interfere in the affairs of others who did not pose a very clear threat. The police would be efficient and effective, but they would only be enforcing a limited set of laws. The courts would be objective and would be about ensuring contracts were enforced. Individuals would be able to enter into any type of voluntary contract (such as gay marriage) or refuse to enter into any contract (as an antigay wedding photographer did with a gay wedding). Adults would be able to take action about which others did not approve, such as smoke marijuana, provided those actions did not violate the rights of others. Religious freedom would prevail, along with all other civil liberties.

Leadership would be focused on individual responsibility. There would be a free market in education with private, for-profit unregulated schools. The successful education models driven by competitive demands would teach students to think critically and to make rational decisions. This educational process would rapidly improve the productivity of the U.S. workforce and create a highly innovative, entrepreneurial environment, which would significantly raise the standard of living.

There would be a role for charity in a classical liberal/libertarian world. However, the role would be limited, because few people would need charity. A proper educational system driven by intense competition would produce productive people with all types of skills and intellectual abilities with a strong work ethic.

The 10 values that would be the foundation of a classical liberal/libertarian society are those that have been outlined in detail in Chapters 3 through 12. In fact, my support for a classical liberal/libertarian political system is derived from the bottom up, not the top down. If these values are the appropriate principles for individuals and if they are the appropriate principles for organizations, by definition they are the appropriate principles for society as a whole. The question then becomes what type of political system is consistent with these principles. The answer is classical liberal/libertarian. The process should begin with asking about the nature of reality (Mother Nature); human nature (a thinking being); the values that will promote the success and happiness of a thinking being, given the laws of Mother Nature; and finally, the political system consistent with these values.

In a classical liberal/libertarian world you cannot have the right to what someone else produces. This would be a violation of that productive person's rights. You cannot have the right to free medical care, because that is the equivalent of enslaving a doctor or enslaving someone else to pay for that doctor. You cannot have the right to someone else's life or their work.

Life, liberty, and the pursuit of happiness captures the vision of the American founders with each individual's moral and exclusive right to his own life, and each individual's fundamental right to be free to pursue his personal happiness—and, by implication, the unconditional right to the product of your labor. If you produce a lot, you get a lot, including the right to give away as much as you want of your production, to whomever you want to, for whatever reason you desire.

Many people of all political persuasions realize liberty is important, but few realize how important it is to human flourishing, both economically and spiritually. In order to think, you must be able to pursue your truth as you know it. If someone forces you to act as if 2 plus 2 equals 5, you literally cannot think. Government rules and regulations often force business decision makers to act as if 2 plus 2 is 5. All human progress is based on creativity and innovation. Innovators must be able to explore new and different ideas, ideas that are often a threat to the status quo. They must be able to think for themselves.

Capitalism (economic freedom) is the only economic/political system that provides the opportunity and incentives to innovate—opportunity in the sense that vested interests cannot protect their territory at the expense of better ideas, and incentives in the sense that those economically productive concepts are rewarded. Not only does this provide incentive income to the innovator, but it also supplies capital through retained earnings. Despite the opposite perception, free markets provide incentives for all the virtues we discussed in Chapters 3 to 12. Free markets discipline irrational and dishonest behavior over the long term.

Obviously there are individuals and organizations that do not demonstrate proper virtues, which survive and sometimes prosper for periods of time. Luck is a factor in life, and Mother Nature is neither just nor unjust. However, over the long term individuals and organizations that demonstrate proper virtues are more likely to prosper in a free market. Free competition reinforces the virtues that are appropriate for individual success. Having the correct virtues improves the probability of success. Therefore, free markets create a self-reinforcing virtuous system. At any point in time there are "bad" individuals and organizations, but the system is constantly disciplining negative behavior. It is a perfect system given human nature, which is neither omnipotent nor omniscient.

Liberty is essential for innovation and creativity, which is the foundation for human physical wellness. Liberty, disciplined by the rule of law, reinforces the principles that are necessary for individual, organizational, and societal well-being.

Liberty is also essential for the pursuit of happiness in the Aristotelian sense of human flourishing. In order to pursue happiness you must be free to live life on your own terms. You must be able to set goals that are personal to you. You must be free to act consistently with your beliefs and your values. Even if you reject the values that have been discussed here, unless you believe in the use of force to justify your ends, you must recognize that to achieve happiness you will need to be free. To deny others their right to freedom deprives them of the opportunity to pursue happiness—to flourish. Being free does not guarantee you will be happy, but if you are not free, you cannot be happy. Freedom and liberty are essential for happiness.

Remember, whenever you support candidates who want to expand the role of government beyond its designated role of protecting individual rights, you are supporting a denial of freedom and liberty—you are supporting a form of slavery.

Liberty is essential for human economic (physical) well-being, and it is also essential for spiritual well-being. Freedom is absolutely necessary for human flourishing. Liberty is not just nice, it is crucial. Be careful when you support the denial of liberty to others and use the "guy with the gun" to support your values, whether these values are progressive/liberal, egalitarian, or religious views on how other adults should behave. It will come back to haunt you.

Let me tell you a story that concretizes the connection of freedom and the pursuit of happiness and why America is a unique and special place. Consider a construction worker, a bricklayer. He has a tough, physically demanding life. My grandfather had that kind of life. This bricklayer has a tough, demanding life, but he and his wife successfully raise their children. Maybe his granddaughter becomes CEO of a publicly traded company. Maybe not. The construction worker has a tough, demanding life, but he gets something incredibly important from his hard work. He gets to be proud of himself. He earns self-esteem from his work.

Consider the same bricklayer and give him welfare. He may be better off materially, but he loses something incredibly important. He loses his pride. He loses his self-esteem. Many people today view the role of government as providing security. This is a false goal. You cannot be secure from reality in the long term, but it is a common goal of government today.

Americans care about security, but the United States is not the land of security. People did not get in small boats and traverse a massive ocean on the way to Jamestown to be secure. America is the land of opportunity—opportunity to be great; opportunity to fail and try again. Most important, the opportunity of that bricklayer is to live life on his own terms, to pursue his personal happiness based on his beliefs and his values, and to live his life as a free and independent person. This is why people come to America. This is the unique American sense of life, which is so precious to protect. This is the concretization of life, liberty, and the pursuit of happiness.

Conclusion

IN THIS BOOK, I ARGUE FOR A SET OF PRINCIPLES THAT IS THE foundation for survival, success, and happiness. These principles are logically derived from the laws of nature (Mother Nature) and human nature. They are applicable to individuals, organizations, and society.

Human beings are goal-directed entities. We have to know where we are going in order to get there. As such, we need a vision (picture) of the future and a purpose consistent with that vision. The vision and purpose act like a beacon and draw us toward who we want to be.

The proper purpose of human beings is to achieve happiness in the Aristotelian context of a life well lived (human flourishing). In other words, it's to achieve blood, sweat, and tears happiness—hard work happiness. When you are 80 years old, you can look back and say, "That was tough, but I am glad I did it."

Everything that is alive has a method of staying alive. A lion has claws to hunt; a deer has speed to avoid the hunter. We have the capacity to think, that is, to reason. Our capacity to think, to be rational, is our only means of survival, success, and happiness. There are no shortcuts or free lunches. Whether this capacity to reason is a result of evolution or is a God-given blessing is not relevant. In either case, the evidence is overwhelming that failing to think rationally, failing to use reason, will have significant negative consequences in the long term.

Reason's nature demands other values. You cannot think rationally unless you are willing to accept reality—the facts. Reason implies thinking logically from the facts of reality. Refusing to accept reality, evasion, is the ultimate psychological sin.

A rational person will think for herself; she will be an independent thinker. Independent thinking implies the opportunity to be creative and innovative and demands personal responsibility.

A rational person will choose to be productive, because productivity is necessary for human survival, given Mother Nature and human nature. Productivity is also a pillar in the pursuit of happiness, which is not surprising, as much (but not all) of our psychological reward system is designed to support our survival. Being productive is healthy, both physically and psychologically.

A rational person will be honest, because honesty is adherence to reality. Being dishonest is being disconnected from reality, which makes it impossible to be rational. The standard for honesty is saying what we mean and knowing what we mean. One of the most destructive forms of dishonesty is claiming knowledge we do not have.

All principles are contextual and for the purpose of promoting one's life and happiness. If someone puts a gun to your head and says, "I will blow your head off unless you tell me I am wonderful," tell him he is wonderful.

Rational people will develop their values outside the "heat of battle." And they will act in a manner consistent with their values in all normal life circumstances (when there is no one with a gun). This is because they know their values will promote their long-term success and happiness. They will act with integrity, not as a duty, but as a means of achieving happiness—of flourishing.

Because other people are essential to your well-being, reason demands that you be just in evaluating others. They should be judged as individuals, based on their personal merits and in the context of the role from which the judgment is being made. Those who contribute the most should receive the most economically and psychologically. Friends can make an enormous contribution to your happiness.

Reason encourages you to establish a self-reward, self-punishment system to remind you to act consistently according to the values that promote your well-being. Pride serves this role by being a psychological reminder to act consistently in accordance with your values (to do good) and a psychological reward for having done well.

Self-esteem fundamentally reflects self-confidence in your ability to live and be successful, given the facts of reality. Because reason is your means of survival and success, acting consistently and rationally raises your self-esteem. In order to have a high level of self-esteem you must believe you have the capacity to be a good person and that you have the moral right to be happy. The most destructive belief in our society is that as human beings we are born bad. This is the most common justification for the use of force to "fix" our behavior.

Everything that is alive must act in its self-interest or die. This is how Mother Nature designed the system. It is not in your rational self-interest to take advantage of other people, because you will not be trusted. On the other hand, you are not required to self-sacrifice. You have as much right to your life as anyone else. If you do not believe you have the right to your own life, by logical extension you must believe no one has a right to his or her own life. And we all become "cannon fodder" for the statists and elitists and their conception of the common good.

The proper moral code for free and prosperous societies, which reflects reason as our means of survival, is to view ourselves as traders. Our goal should be to figure out how to get better together. Rationality demands that we focus on creating as many win-win relationships as possible. Win-lose and lose-win relationships always ultimately become lose-lose.

Reason demands that you pursue your long-term rational self-interest properly understood. This requires that you have a sense of purpose, take care of your body, take care of your mind, and work to create meaningful relationships with individuals who share your values. The real problem in the world is not that people pursue their long-term rational self-interest, but that many people are self-destructive, at least in some aspect of their lives.

Reason also requires that you let others also act accordingly. Most complex activities are accomplished in teams of one form or another. If teamwork is necessary for the accomplishment of your purpose, reason demands you be an effective team player. This requires you to do your job well, work with your fellow teammates in a mutually supportive manner, and understand how your work impacts the rest of the team.

The task of self-leadership is to be clear about your vision, purpose, and values for promoting your survival, success, and happiness— to flourish.

The principles that are applicable to individuals are the same as for organizations. In reality, there are only individuals; organizations are simply individuals working together. Organizational leadership is about the integration of the skills, knowledge, and behavior of the members of the organizations consistent with the vision, purpose, and values of the organization. The goal is logical consistency. People cannot act consistently with inconsistent goals or values. Integration is based on effective concept formation and is an important aspect of rational thinking—that is, reason.

The principles that are applicable to individuals are also applicable to society. Again, there are only individuals in reality. Society is simply individuals living together. In this context, there is practically no such thing as the common good. Almost any decision is good for some people and not good for others, or at least not of equal impact to all. The only common good consistent with every individual's pursuit of her or his happiness is the prevention of the initiation of force. All other forms of common good violate the rights of someone.

The Founding Fathers of the United States were fundamentally influenced by the thinkers of the Enlightenment—the Age of Reason. Although they had mixed premises, they were primarily advocates of liberty. They realized that freedom was essential for human flourishing. They viewed the role of government as fundamentally to protect individual rights. Government was therefore to be limited. It was not designed to eliminate all supposed ills. Voluntary relations were the source of problem resolutions. They realized that the abuse of power by government was inevitable if it was not controlled and limited.

The United States is not a democracy, despite the claims by both Democratic and Republican politicians to the contrary. The United States is a constitutional republic based on the protection of individual rights. If we were a democracy, we would have perished long ago. One of the great fears of the Founders was the "tyranny of the majority"—the ability of the majority to violate the rights of individuals, and ultimately the ability of the majority to vote a "free lunch" for themselves. When 51 percent of the population find out they can vote a free lunch from 49 percent, fairly soon the party is over. Because shortly thereafter, 60 percent want a free lunch from 40 percent, then 70 percent want a free lunch from 30 percent, and finally the 30 percent quit. This scenario always leads to tyranny of one kind or another.

Only in a free society can an individual pursue her personal happiness in a manner consistent with the principles we have discussed. In addition, a free society nurtures and reinforces these principles.

Concepts such as honesty, integrity, rationality, and personal responsibility are all rewarded in a free society. The competition of ideas and results drives individuals to act rationally in free markets and free societies. Naturally, there will always be some deviant behavior, because human beings have free will. But the incentive structure in free societies rewards strong moral character, and moral behavior is the societal norm when the initiation of force is prohibited.

Values matter for individuals, organizations, and society as a whole. A society based on the correct ideals will flourish. It is critical that we return to the principles that made America great—life, liberty, and the pursuit of happiness.

Index

Acknowledgments

I SHOULD BEGIN BY ACKNOWLEDGING MY GREATER FAMILY, WHO are typical middle class, hardworking, honest individuals who exemplify the American sense of life. I am blessed with a tremendously supportive wife, Betty, of 41 years, who makes my life meaningful, and three great children, Eric, William, and Sarah.

It is also appropriate to thank the outstanding employees at BB&T and the Cato Institute who have made me "look good." I especially am fortunate to have worked with the executive management team who built BB&T: Ken Chalk, Kelly King, Scott Reed, and Henry Williamson. I owe Ed Crane and Charles Koch a thank you for creating and growing Cato. The faculty at Wake Forest Business School, and especially Dean Steve Reinemund, are an outstanding group, as are the students. They provided me with a meaningful educational experience.

My deepest intellectual debts are to Aristotle, Ayn Rand, and Leonard Peikoff. Rand's ideas created a new world view for me and fundamentally made this book possible. Leonard Peikoff's book, *Objectivism: The Philosophy of Ayn Rand*, enabled me to integrate Rand's philosophy and successfully apply it to my work and life.

My longtime executive assistant, Gail Flowers, and my current executive assistant, Beth Santos, were essential by typing and interpreting my handwritten manuscript. Some think I took writing lessons from my family physician, but my writing is much harder to read than most doctors' handwriting.

The staff at McGraw-Hill is a pleasure to work with, especially my editor, Donya Dickerson. They clearly demonstrate the win-win relationship concept.

About the Author

 **John A. Allison** is currently president and CEO of the Cato Institute, the global leading libertarian "think tank." Previously, Allison served for 20 years as chairman and CEO of BB&T, one of the largest financial institutions in the United States. Allison is a former Distinguished Professor of Practice at Wake Forest University. He received a Lifetime Achievement Award from the *American Banker* and was named one of the decade's top 100 most successful CEOs in the world by the *Harvard Business Review*. Allison is the recipient of six honorary doctorate degrees and is the author of the *New York Times* bestselling book *The Financial Crisis and the Free Market Cure*.